I0446725

Passive Income Starter Guide:
Building Wealth for Beginners

MG Horizons Editions

TABLE OF CONTENTS

INTRODUCTION:
"Passive Income Starter Guide" is a comprehensive book designed for beginners who want to escape the 9-to-5 grind and embark on the journey of financial freedom. This guide provides step-by-step instructions, practical strategies, and real-life examples to help readers understand the concept of passive income and create sustainable revenue streams.

CHAPTER 1:
UNDERSTANDING PASSIVE INCOME

Introduction: Unshackling from the 9-to-5
Welcome to the world of financial freedom, where your money works for you, and you're no longer a slave to the traditional 9-to-5 grind. In this chapter, we'll embark on a journey to understand the essence of passive income and how it can transform your life. It's not just about earning money while you sleep; it's about reclaiming your time, empowering your choices, and securing your future.

1.1 Defining Passive Income: Beyond the Conventional Paycheck
We'll demystify the term 'passive income,' breaking it down to its core. Learn why passive income is not just a buzzword but a fundamental shift in the way you perceive earning.

1.2 The Benefits of Passive Income: More Than Just Money
Explore the multifaceted advantages of passive income. From financial security to flexibility and reduced stress, discover how passive income impacts various aspects of your life.

1.3 Debunking Myths: Separating Fact from Fiction
Address common misconceptions about passive income. We'll unveil the truth behind the myths and clarify unrealistic expectations, setting a realistic foundation for your journey.

1.4 Active vs. Passive Income: Understanding the Difference
Distinguish between active and passive income sources. Understand why the traditional 'active' methods might not be sustainable in the long run and why passive income offers a smarter alternative.

1.5 The Mindset Shift: Cultivating the Passive Income Mentality
Success in the passive income realm requires a different mindset. Learn the essential mindset shifts necessary to embrace opportunities, overcome challenges, and persist in your pursuit of financial freedom.

1.6 Assessing Your Financial Goals: Defining Your Path

Identify your financial goals and aspirations. We'll guide you through exercises to help you set clear, achievable objectives, ensuring your passive income endeavors align with your life's ambitions.

1.7 The Road Ahead: What to Expect

Get a sneak peek into the chapters to come. Understand the structure of this book and how each section contributes to your understanding of passive income. Brace yourself for transformative insights and actionable strategies that lie ahead.

Key Takeaways:

• Passive income is not just about money; it's about reclaiming time and choices.
• Understanding the difference between active and passive income is crucial for making informed decisions.
• Embracing the right mindset is as important as the strategies themselves.
• Defining your financial goals sets the foundation for your passive income journey.

In the following chapters, we'll delve deeper into specific passive income streams, providing you with the knowledge and tools needed to take your first steps towards financial independence. Are you ready to embark on this empowering journey? Let's begin.

1.1 DEFINING PASSIVE INCOME: BEYOND THE CONVENTIONAL PAYCHECK

In the realm of traditional employment, the equation is simple: time equals money. You work a certain number of hours, and at the end of the week or month, you receive a paycheck. This direct correlation between your time and your earnings forms the basis of active income.

Passive income, on the other hand, operates on an entirely different principle. At its core, passive income is money earned with little to no effort on your part. It's the art of making your money work for you, rather than you working for money. Unlike active income, where your revenue stream stops the moment you stop working, passive income continues to flow, even when you're asleep, traveling the world, or spending quality time with your loved ones.

But here's the magic: passive income doesn't mean no work at all. It means you put in the effort upfront or maintain a system, and then it generates income without requiring constant, active involvement. This upfront effort can involve creating a product, investing in assets, building a business, or acquiring specialized knowledge that is in demand.

Examples of Passive Income:

1. Royalties from Intellectual Property: If you're a writer, musician, or artist, you can earn royalties whenever your work is sold or used.

2. Investment Income: Earnings from investments in stocks, bonds, mutual funds, or real estate properties can generate regular passive income through dividends, interest, or rental payments.

3. Online Businesses: Creating and monetizing a blog, YouTube channel, or an e-commerce store can generate passive income through ads, affiliate marketing, or product sales, once the initial setup and content creation are done.

4. Rental Properties: Owning and renting out properties can provide a steady stream of passive income after deducting expenses like maintenance and property management.

5. Automated Online Courses: Developing online courses or digital products and automating the sales and delivery processes can generate passive income as long as the content remains relevant and valuable.

Understanding this fundamental shift from trading time for money to creating systems that generate income independently is the cornerstone of passive income. As we delve deeper into various passive income streams in this book, you'll discover the strategies and methods to create these systems, allowing you to craft your path toward financial freedom.

1.2 THE BENEFITS OF PASSIVE INCOME: MORE THAN JUST MONEY

Passive income isn't just a financial concept; it's a lifestyle choice that can reshape every aspect of your life. Let's explore the diverse array of benefits that passive income offers, extending far beyond mere monetary gains:

Financial Security:
With multiple streams of passive income, you create a safety net that traditional jobs can't provide. Financial shocks, unexpected expenses, or sudden job loss become manageable hurdles rather than insurmountable crises.

Time Freedom:
The most precious commodity in life is time. Passive income liberates your time, allowing you to focus on what truly matters – be it spending time with family, pursuing hobbies, traveling, or furthering your education. Your money works tirelessly, affording you the luxury of choice.

Reduced Stress and Burnout:
Traditional jobs often come with stress and burnout due to demanding schedules and pressure. Passive income reduces the dependency on a single income source, alleviating the stress associated with living paycheck to paycheck.

Flexibility and Mobility:
Passive income isn't bound by geographical constraints. With online passive income streams, you can work from anywhere in the world. This flexibility opens opportunities for travel, relocation, and exploring new cultures, all while your income continues to flow.

Wealth Accumulation:
By reinvesting your passive income, you can accelerate wealth accumulation. Whether it's through investments, expanding your business, or acquiring new income-generating assets, your money compounds, steadily increasing your net worth over time.

Entrepreneurial Opportunities:

With stable passive income, you have the freedom to explore entrepreneurial ventures. You can invest in startups, mentor others, or even start passion projects without the fear of financial instability.

Quality of Life Improvement:

Passive income can improve your overall quality of life. It can fund your children's education, allow you to live in a better neighborhood, and provide access to healthcare and experiences that enhance your well-being.

Generational Wealth and Legacy:

Passive income allows you to build generational wealth. By passing down your knowledge, assets, and income streams, you create a lasting legacy for your family, ensuring financial security for future generations.

Personal Fulfillment:

Creating and managing passive income streams based on your interests and passions can be deeply fulfilling. It allows you to align your work with your values, leading to a sense of purpose and fulfillment in your endeavors.

Conclusion:

The benefits of passive income extend far beyond monetary gains, encompassing freedom, flexibility, and fulfillment. By understanding these advantages, you're not just embarking on a journey to financial independence but also opening the door to a life rich in experiences, opportunities, and personal fulfillment. As we delve into the strategies and techniques in the subsequent chapters, keep these profound benefits in mind – they are the driving force behind your pursuit of passive income.

1.3 DEBUNKING MYTHS: SEPARATING FACT FROM FICTION

Passive income, while an exciting prospect, often comes with its fair share of misconceptions and myths that can mislead aspiring entrepreneurs. In this section, we'll unravel these myths, ensuring you approach your passive income journey with clear and realistic expectations.

Myth 1: Passive Income Requires No Effort
Fact: While the term "passive" might suggest no effort, the reality is that setting up and maintaining passive income streams requires substantial effort, especially in the beginning. Whether it's creating a product, building a website, or marketing your services, there's groundwork to be done. The difference is that the effort is front-loaded; once established, passive income requires less day-to-day effort than a traditional job.

Myth 2: Passive Income Guarantees Overnight Wealth
Fact: Building a sustainable passive income takes time and patience. Overnight success stories are rare and often the result of extensive prior effort. Realistic expectations are essential. It's a journey that requires consistent dedication and a willingness to learn from failures along the way.

Myth 3: Passive Income is Completely Risk-Free
Fact: All investments, including passive income ventures, come with inherent risks. Markets fluctuate, businesses face competition, and economic factors can impact income streams. Understanding and managing risks is crucial. Diversification and continuous learning can mitigate many potential pitfalls.

Myth 4: You Need a Lot of Money to Start
Fact: While having capital can speed up the process, many passive income streams, especially online ventures, can be started with minimal investment. What's often more critical is your time, effort, and creativity. Smart financial planning and leveraging available resources can help you kick-start your passive income journey without a hefty initial investment.

Myth 5: Passive Income is Only for Experts
Fact: Thanks to the internet and numerous online resources, anyone can learn and venture into passive income. You don't need a specific degree or decades of experience. A willingness to learn, adapt, and apply knowledge is more important. Countless beginners have built successful passive income streams through dedication and continuous learning.

Myth 6: Passive Income Is Not Taxable

Fact: Passive income is generally taxable. Understanding tax implications is crucial to avoid legal issues. Different income streams may have varying tax structures. It's advisable to consult a tax professional to ensure compliance with tax regulations.

Conclusion:

By dispelling these myths, we pave the way for a realistic understanding of passive income. It's not a magic formula but a proven method for financial independence when approached with diligence, determination, and an informed mindset. Armed with this knowledge, you're better equipped to navigate the exciting path ahead and build your passive income empire.

1.4 ACTIVE VS. PASSIVE INCOME: UNDERSTANDING THE DIFFERENCE

In the world of earning, there are two fundamental approaches: active income and passive income. Understanding the distinctions between these models is pivotal as you embark on your journey to financial freedom.

Active Income: Trading Time for Money

Active income represents the conventional method of earning, where you exchange your time and expertise for money. This is the essence of most traditional jobs. You work for a specific number of hours, and in return, you receive a paycheck. Doctors, lawyers, teachers, and employees in various fields earn active income. The key features of active income include:

- Direct Effort: You need to be actively involved in the work to get paid. If you stop working, your income stops.
- Limited Scalability: Your earning potential is capped by the number of hours you can work. As there are only 24 hours in a day, there's a limit to how much you can earn.
- Time Dependency: You must continually invest time to maintain your income. Vacations or sick days can directly impact your earnings.

Passive Income: Making Money Work for You

Passive income, in stark contrast, is money earned with little to no active involvement. It's the art of making your money work for you. Once the initial effort, investment, or setup is complete, passive income streams continue to generate revenue with minimal ongoing effort. Key aspects of passive income include:

- Front-Loaded Effort: Significant effort is required upfront, whether in creating a product, building a business, or investing. This effort is often followed by periods of maintenance and occasional adjustments.

- Scalability: Passive income is highly scalable. Once established, it can grow exponentially without proportional increases in your time and effort.
- Time Freedom: Passive income liberates your time, allowing you to pursue other interests, invest in personal growth, or create additional income streams.

Understanding the Hybrid Model

Many successful individuals adopt a hybrid approach, combining active and passive income streams. For instance, a writer may earn active income from freelance work while simultaneously generating passive income from book royalties. This hybrid model provides financial stability while building long-term wealth.

Conclusion: The Path to Financial Freedom

Recognizing the distinctions between active and passive income is the first step toward financial freedom. As you progress through this book, you'll delve deeper into specific passive income streams and learn how to transition from trading time for money to building income systems that work tirelessly, affording you the life you desire. Embrace this knowledge and set the stage for your transformative journey to financial independence.

1.5 THE MINDSET SHIFT:
CULTIVATING THE PASSIVE INCOME MENTALITY

Beyond the practicalities of passive income lies a profound shift in mindset, a transformation that can reshape your approach to work, money, and life itself. Cultivating the passive income mentality is not just about financial strategies; it's about adopting a new way of thinking and perceiving the world. Here's how to nurture this transformative mindset:

1.Embrace Creativity and Innovation:

In the realm of passive income, creativity knows no bounds. Cultivate a mindset that welcomes innovation and new ideas. Be open to exploring unconventional paths and thinking outside the box. The most successful passive income entrepreneurs are often those who dare to innovate and create something unique.

2. Develop a Long-Term Perspective:

Passive income is a journey, not a sprint. Cultivate patience and perseverance. Understand that building sustainable income streams takes time, effort, and consistent dedication. Keep your long-term goals in focus and avoid the lure of get-rich-quick schemes.

3. Embrace Failure as a Stepping Stone:

Failure is not the end; it's a crucial part of the learning process. Cultivate resilience and view failures as valuable lessons. Every setback is an opportunity to refine your approach, learn, and grow. Embracing failure as a natural part of the entrepreneurial journey can lead to eventual success.

4. Develop a Growth Mindset:

A growth mindset thrives on challenges and sees effort as a path to mastery. Cultivate the belief that your abilities and intelligence can be developed with dedication and hard work. View challenges as opportunities to learn and improve. This mindset fosters adaptability and a willingness to embrace change, vital qualities in the ever-evolving world of passive income.

5. Foster a Wealth Consciousness:

Shift your beliefs about money and abundance. Cultivate an attitude of abundance rather than scarcity. Recognize that there are abundant opportunities and in the world, and your ability to tap into them is not limited. A positive mindset about wealth can attract opportunities and create a mindset conducive to financial success.

6. Practice Automation and Delegation:

Develop the habit of automating repetitive tasks and delegating responsibilities. Cultivate the mindset of working smarter, not harder. Understand that your time is precious, and by automating and delegating, you free yourself to focus on strategic decisions and high-value tasks, maximizing your efficiency.

Conclusion: The Power of Mindset in Passive Income Success

Cultivating the passive income mentality is not just about financial gain; it's about personal growth and empowerment. By adopting these principles and embracing the entrepreneurial mindset, you lay a solid foundation for your passive income ventures. As you progress through this book, remember that your mindset is as crucial as your strategies. It's the driving force that can turn challenges into opportunities and dreams into reality. Cultivate this mindset, and you'll find yourself well-equipped for the exciting journey ahead.

1.6 ASSESSING YOUR FINANCIAL GOALS: DEFINING YOUR PATH

Before you embark on your passive income journey, it's crucial to have a clear understanding of your financial goals. Your goals act as a roadmap, guiding your decisions and shaping your passive income strategies. In this section, you'll learn how to assess and define your financial objectives.

1. Reflect on Your Why:
Begin by asking yourself why you want to generate passive income. Is it to achieve financial freedom, travel the world, fund your children's education, or retire early? Understanding your motivations provides clarity and purpose to your efforts.

2. Set Specific, Measurable Goals:
Vague goals like "I want to make more money" won't suffice. Instead, set specific and measurable goals. For instance, "I want to generate $5,000 per month in passive income within two years." Specific goals provide a clear target to work towards.

3. Prioritize Your Goals:
List your financial goals in order of priority. Determine which goals are short-term (achievable within one to two years), medium-term (three to five years), and long-term (more than five years). Prioritizing your goals helps you allocate resources effectively.

4. Calculate Your Financial Freedom Number:
Your financial freedom number is the amount of passive income required to cover your living expenses and achieve your desired lifestyle. Calculate your monthly expenses and multiply them by 12 to get your annual expenses. Multiply this figure by 25 (based on the 4% rule) to estimate the capital needed to generate that income passively.

5. Consider Risk Tolerance:
Evaluate your risk tolerance level. Some passive income streams, like stocks or real estate, come with certain risks. Determine how much risk you're comfortable with and align your investment choices accordingly.

6. Account for Inflation and Emergency Funds:

Factor in inflation when setting your financial goals. The purchasing power of money decreases over time due to inflation, so your passive income should grow to keep pace with rising costs. Additionally, build an emergency fund to cover unforeseen expenses, ensuring your passive income remains unaffected during financial emergencies.

7. Review and Adjust Regularly:

Financial goals are not set in stone. Life circumstances change, and so should your goals. Regularly review your goals, assess your progress, and make adjustments as necessary. Celebrate milestones and use them as motivation to keep moving forward.

Conclusion: Your Roadmap to Financial Freedom

By assessing your financial goals, you create a roadmap that directs your passive income efforts. Clarity about your objectives empowers you to make informed decisions, choose appropriate income streams, and stay focused on the path to financial freedom. As you proceed through this book, keep your goals in mind; they are the driving force behind your journey to a life of financial independence and abundance.

1.7 THE ROAD AHEAD:
WHAT TO EXPECT

Congratulations on laying the groundwork for your passive income journey. As you step onto this transformative path, it's essential to understand what lies ahead and what you can expect from this exciting venture.

1. Continuous Learning and Adaptation:

The world of passive income is dynamic and ever-changing. New opportunities, technologies, and strategies constantly emerge. Embrace the mindset of a perpetual learner. Stay updated with industry trends, attend webinars, read books, and engage with communities. The willingness to adapt and evolve your strategies is key to long-term success.

2. Initial Challenges and Learning Curves:

In the early stages, you might face challenges and encounter learning curves. This is normal. Building passive income streams, especially for beginners, requires patience, persistence, and a willingness to overcome obstacles. Each challenge is a learning opportunity that propels you toward expertise.

3. Time and Effort Investment:

While the goal of passive income is to reduce active involvement, the initial setup demands time, effort, and dedication. Be prepared to invest your energy in researching, planning, and executing your strategies. Your hard work during the setup phase paves the way for a more streamlined and automated income flow later on.

4. Diversification and Risk Management:

Diversifying your passive income streams is a prudent strategy. Relying on a single source of income can be risky. Spread your investments and efforts across different streams, minimizing the impact of potential setbacks in one area. Additionally, practice effective risk management and be aware of potential pitfalls.

5. Building a Supportive Network:

Surround yourself with a supportive network of mentors, peers, and like-minded individuals. Engage with online communities, attend networking events, and seek guidance from experienced passive income entrepreneurs. A supportive network can provide valuable insights, motivation, and solutions to challenges you might face.

6. Celebrating Milestones:

Acknowledge and celebrate your achievements, no matter how small they may seem. Whether it's your first affiliate sale, book publication, or successful investment, these milestones signify your progress. Celebrating them not only boosts your morale but also reinforces your commitment to your passive income journey.

7. Financial Freedom and Empowerment:

As your passive income streams grow, you'll begin to experience financial freedom. Your income becomes less reliant on your active participation, allowing you the freedom to pursue your passions, spend time with loved ones, and explore new opportunities. This empowerment is one of the most rewarding aspects of the passive income journey.

Conclusion: Your Journey Begins

The road ahead is both challenging and rewarding. As you navigate the twists and turns, keep your goals, mindset, and perseverance at the forefront. Your journey toward financial freedom and a life of abundance is underway. Remember, every step you take brings you closer to the life you've envisioned. Embrace the challenges, learn from them, and celebrate your victories. Your passive income adventure starts now. Safe travels!

CHAPTER 2:
BUILDING A STRONG FINANCIAL FOUNDATION

Introduction: The Bedrock of Financial Freedom
Before diving into the intricacies of passive income, it's crucial to build a robust financial foundation. This chapter serves as the cornerstone of your journey toward financial freedom. By understanding the basics of personal finance, managing your money effectively, and cultivating healthy financial habits, you'll be better equipped to make informed decisions about your passive income ventures.

2.1 Mastering Budgeting and Expense Management:
- Explore the art of budgeting: creating a budget, tracking expenses, and identifying discretionary and non-discretionary spending.
- Understand the significance of living below your means and how it contributes to financial stability.
- Learn practical strategies for reducing expenses without compromising your quality of life.

2.2 The Importance of Emergency Funds:
- Delve into the concept of emergency funds and why they are your financial safety net.
- Determine the ideal size of an emergency fund based on your lifestyle and responsibilities.
- Explore where to store your emergency fund for accessibility and growth.

2.3 Debt Management and Elimination Strategies:
- Understand different types of debts, their impact on your financial health, and good vs. bad debt.
- Learn debt elimination techniques such as the snowball and avalanche methods.
- Explore debt consolidation and refinancing options to make repayment more manageable.

2.4 Investing in Your Future:
• Explore the significance of retirement planning and the power of compound interest.
• Understand different retirement accounts like 401(k), IRA, and Roth IRA and choose the best option for your circumstances.
• Learn about employer matching, vesting periods, and how to maximize your retirement contributions.

2.5 Smart Saving and Investment Strategies:
• Discover the importance of saving for short-term goals and emergencies while investing for long-term wealth.
• Explore various investment vehicles, including stocks, bonds, mutual funds, real estate, and index funds.
• Learn about risk tolerance, asset allocation, and how to create a diversified investment portfolio.

2.6 Tax Efficiency and Financial Planning:
• Understand the basics of tax planning, deductions, and credits to optimize your tax situation.
• Learn about tax-efficient investment strategies and the impact of taxes on your investment returns.
• Explore the role of financial advisors and tax professionals in comprehensive financial planning.

Conclusion: Your Financial Roadmap
Building a strong financial foundation is not just about managing money; it's about creating a roadmap to achieve your goals. In this chapter, you've laid the groundwork for your financial future. Armed with a solid understanding of budgeting, emergency funds, debt management, investing, and tax efficiency, you're now ready to explore the world of passive income with confidence. As you move forward, remember that a strong financial foundation is the bedrock upon which your passive income empire will flourish. Stay committed to these principles, and you'll be well on your way to financial freedom.

2.1 MASTERING BUDGETING AND EXPENSE MANAGEMENT:

Understanding the Art of Budgeting:

Budgeting is the cornerstone of financial stability. It's not just about tracking your expenses; it's a tool that empowers you to take control of your finances. By creating a budget, you gain insights into your spending habits and can make informed decisions about where your money goes. Here's how to master the art of budgeting:

- Creating a Budget: Start by listing your sources of income and all your monthly expenses. Categorize your expenses into fixed (e.g., rent, mortgage) and variable (e.g., groceries, entertainment). Use budgeting apps or spreadsheets to organize this information.
- Tracking Expenses: Regularly monitor your spending. Track every purchase, no matter how small. This awareness is key to identifying unnecessary expenditures and making adjustments to your budget.
- Differentiating Between Needs and Wants: Distinguish between essential expenses (needs) and discretionary spending (wants). While needs are non-negotiable, wants can be trimmed to allocate more funds toward savings and investments.

Living Below Your Means:

Living below your means is a fundamental principle of financial stability. It means your expenses are less than your income, allowing you to save and invest. Here's how to achieve this balance:

- Avoid Lifestyle Inflation: As your income increases, resist the urge to inflate your lifestyle proportionally. Instead, direct the additional income toward savings, investments, and debt reduction.
- Frugal Living: Embrace frugality by being mindful of your spending. Look for discounts, buy used items, and cook at home. Small savings accumulate over time, bolstering your financial foundation.

Reducing Expenses Without Sacrificing Quality of Life:

Reducing expenses doesn't mean sacrificing your quality of life. It's about making conscious choices and finding cost-effective alternatives:

- Cutting Unnecessary Subscriptions: Review your subscriptions, be it streaming services, magazines, or memberships. Cancel those you don't fully utilize.
- Negotiating Bills: Negotiate with service providers for better deals on utilities, internet, and insurance. Loyalty often leads to discounts.
- Smart Shopping: Compare prices before making significant purchases. Use cashback apps and take advantage of sales and discounts to get the best deals.

Conclusion: Empowering Your Financial Future

Mastering budgeting and expense management isn't about restricting yourself; it's about freeing yourself from financial stress. By understanding where your money goes and making conscious choices, you gain control over your financial destiny. This newfound control sets the stage for effective saving, investing, and ultimately, passive income generation. As you move forward, carry these budgeting skills with you; they will serve as the backbone of your financial success.

2.2 THE IMPORTANCE OF EMERGENCY FUNDS:

Understanding the Safety Net:

Life is unpredictable, and financial emergencies can arise unexpectedly. An emergency fund acts as your financial safety net, providing a cushion to fall back on during challenging times. Here's how to understand and build a robust emergency fund:

- Defining an Emergency: An emergency is an unforeseen event that requires immediate financial attention, such as medical expenses, car repairs, or unexpected job loss. It's essential to differentiate between emergencies and planned expenses.
- Determining the Ideal Size: The size of your emergency fund depends on your lifestyle, expenses, and job stability. Financial experts often recommend saving three to six months' worth of living expenses. Consider factors like dependents, job security, and health when calculating the appropriate amount.

Where to Store Your Emergency Fund:

Where you store your emergency fund impacts accessibility and growth potential. While it should be easily accessible, it should also earn some interest to beat inflation:

- High-Yield Savings Account: A high-yield savings account offers better interest rates than regular savings accounts. It's easily accessible, ensuring you can withdraw funds in emergencies.
- Money Market Account: Money market accounts provide higher interest rates than regular savings accounts and often come with limited check-writing abilities, making them a viable option for emergency funds.
- Certificates of Deposit (CDs): CDs offer higher interest rates than savings accounts, but your money is locked in for a specific period. Choose CDs with terms that align with the likelihood of needing the funds in an emergency.

Regular Contributions and Maintenance:

Building an emergency fund is not a one-time task; it requires consistent effort and dedication:

- Automate Savings: Set up automatic transfers to your emergency fund each month. Treating it as a non-negotiable expense ensures consistent contributions.
- Periodic Reviews: Regularly review and adjust your emergency fund based on changes in your lifestyle, expenses, and income. Reassess your fund's size during major life events like marriage, childbirth, or career changes.

Conclusion: Financial Peace of Mind

An emergency fund is not just a financial asset; it's peace of mind in a crisis. By understanding its importance and diligently building and maintaining it, you shield yourself from the financial stress that emergencies can bring. This fund not only provides stability but also acts as a foundation upon which you can confidently build your passive income ventures. Cultivate the habit of saving, and your emergency fund will stand as a testament to your financial preparedness.

2.3 DEBT MANAGEMENT AND ELIMINATION STRATEGIES:

Understanding Different Types of Debt:

Not all debts are created equal. It's crucial to differentiate between good debt (such as a mortgage or student loans) and bad debt (like high-interest credit card debt). Understanding the types of debt you have helps you make informed decisions about managing and eliminating them.

- Good Debt vs. Bad Debt: Good debt contributes to your financial growth, often with low interest rates and potential tax benefits. Bad debt, on the other hand, has high-interest rates and can quickly become burdensome.

Debt Elimination Techniques:

Eliminating debt is a pivotal step toward financial freedom. Consider these effective debt elimination strategies:

- Snowball Method: List your debts from smallest to largest, regardless of interest rates. Pay the minimum on all debts but focus extra funds on the smallest debt. Once it's paid off, roll that payment into the next smallest debt. This method provides psychological victories, motivating you to tackle larger debts.

- Avalanche Method: List your debts by interest rate, from highest to lowest. Allocate extra funds to the debt with the highest interest rate while paying the minimum on others. Once the high-interest debt is paid off, move to the next highest interest rate. This method minimizes the total interest paid overtime.
- Debt Consolidation: Consider consolidating high-interest debts into a single, lower-interest loan. Debt consolidation simplifies payments and reduces the overall interest burden, making it easier to pay off debt faster.

Debt Refinancing and Negotiation:
- Refinancing: Explore refinancing options for high-interest loans, especially student loans or mortgages. Lowering the interest rate can significantly reduce your monthly payments and the overall amount you repay over time.
- Negotiating with Creditors: If you're struggling with credit card debt, contact your creditors to negotiate lower interest rates or set up a manageable payment plan. Many creditors are willing to work with you to recover the debt, avoiding more drastic measures like collections or charge-offs.

Avoiding Debt Pitfalls:
- Credit Card Discipline: Use credit cards responsibly. Pay the full balance monthly to avoid interest charges. If you can't pay in full, have a clear plan to pay off the balance promptly.
- Emergency Fund: Maintain a robust emergency fund to avoid relying on credit cards or loans in emergencies, preventing the accumulation of high-interest debt.

Conclusion: Freedom from Financial Burden
By understanding the nuances of debt and employing effective elimination strategies, you're not just eradicating financial liabilities; you're freeing yourself from the stress and constraints that debt brings. Becoming debt-free opens doors to investing, saving, and ultimately, generating passive income. Your journey to financial freedom begins with managing and eliminating debt strategically and responsibly.

2.4 INVESTING IN YOUR FUTURE:

The Significance of Retirement Planning:
Planning for your retirement is not just a prudent choice; it's a necessity. As life expectancy increases, a well-funded retirement plan ensures you maintain your quality of life after you stop working. Here's how to secure your golden years:

- Understanding Compound Interest: The earlier you start saving, the more your money can grow through compound interest. Compound interest allows your initial investment to earn interest, and then, over time, it earns interest on both the principal and the accumulated interest, leading to exponential growth.
- Types of Retirement Accounts: Explore retirement accounts like 401(k)s, IRAs, and Roth IRAs. Understand their tax advantages, contribution limits, and withdrawal rules. Contribute consistently and take advantage of employer matches if available.

Employer Matching and Vesting:
- Understanding Employer Matching: Some employers match your contributions up to a certain percentage of your salary. This is essentially free money. Contribute at least enough to get the full match – it's an instant return on your investment.
- Vesting Periods: Be aware of vesting schedules. You might not fully own employer-contributed funds until you've worked for the company for a specific period. Understand these terms to make informed decisions about your employment and retirement planning.

Smart Investment Choices:
- Diversification: Diversify your investments across different asset classes such as stocks, bonds, and real estate. Diversification spreads risk, protecting your investments from the fluctuations of a single market.
- Risk Tolerance: Assess your risk tolerance. Stocks offer high returns but come with higher volatility. Bonds provide stability but lower returns. Allocate your investments based on your comfort with risk and your investment timeline.

Regular Reviews and Adjustments:
- Periodic Portfolio Review: Regularly review your investment portfolio. Rebalance your assets if necessary to maintain your desired risk level. Consider allocating investments as you approach retirement to protect your capital.
- Consulting Financial Advisors: Consider consulting a financial advisor, especially if your investments are complex or you lack the expertise.

A professional can provide personalized advice tailored to your financial goals and risk tolerance.

Conclusion: Securing Your Financial Legacy

Investing in your future is not just about accumulating wealth; it's about securing your financial legacy and ensuring a comfortable retirement. By understanding the power of compound interest, leveraging employer matches, making smart investment choices, and regularly reviewing your portfolio, you're setting the stage for a financially secure future. Your investments are the seeds of your passive income, growing steadily over time and providing the support you need in your retirement years. Start early, invest wisely, and your future self will thank you.

2.5 SMART SAVING AND INVESTMENT STRATEGIES:

The Importance of Short-Term and Long-Term Financial Goals:

- Short-Term Goals: Identify and save for short-term financial goals such as building an emergency fund, taking a vacation, or buying a car. Allocate funds specifically for these goals to ensure you don't dip into your long-term investments.
- Long-Term Goals: Long-term goals, such as purchasing a home, funding your children's education, or retiring comfortably, require strategic investment planning. Understand the timeline for these goals and choose investment options that align with your objectives.

Saving Strategies:

- Automated Savings: Set up automated transfers to your savings accounts. Automating your savings ensures consistency and discipline in your saving habits. Treat your savings like any other non-negotiable monthly expense.
- Windfall Allocation: Allocate windfalls like tax refunds, bonuses, or unexpected inheritances to your savings or investment accounts. While it might be tempting to splurge, redirecting windfalls toward your financial goals accelerates your progress.

Investment Vehicles:

- Stock Market Investments: Invest in stocks for long-term growth. Consider index funds and mutual funds for diversification. Historically, the stock market has provided substantial returns over the long term.
- Real Estate: Real estate investments, such as rental properties, can provide a steady income stream and appreciate over time. Research local markets and property types before making investment decisions.

Risk Management and Diversification:

- Risk Management: Assess your risk tolerance before investing. Understand that higher returns often come with higher risks. Diversify your investments across different asset classes to spread risk and minimize potential losses.
- Regular Monitoring: Regularly monitor your investments. Stay informed about market trends, economic indicators, and geopolitical events that can impact your investments. Adjust your portfolio as needed to align with your risk tolerance and financial goals.

Educational Investments:

- Continuous Learning: Invest in your financial education. Read books, attend workshops, and take online courses to enhance your knowledge of personal finance and investment strategies. Knowledge is a powerful tool in making informed investment decisions.

Conclusion: Growing Your Wealth Strategically

Smart saving and investment strategies are the building blocks of your financial empire. By setting clear goals, automating your savings, choosing diverse investment vehicles, and staying informed, you're not just growing your wealth; you're ensuring its stability and long-term growth. As you implement these strategies, you're one step closer to generating passive income that can sustain your desired lifestyle. Remember, smart financial choices today pave the way for a prosperous tomorrow.

2.6 TAX EFFICIENCY
AND FINANCIAL PLANNING:

Understanding the Basics of Tax Planning:

- Tax Deductions: Familiarize yourself with available tax deductions such as mortgage interest, student loan interest, and contributions to retirement accounts. Utilize these deductions to reduce your taxable income.
- Tax Credits: Explore tax credits like the Earned Income Tax Credit (EITC) and Child Tax Credit. Credits directly reduce your tax liability, providing substantial savings. Ensure you qualify for these credits and claim them when filing your taxes.

Tax-Efficient Investment Strategies:

- Tax-Advantaged Accounts: Maximize contributions to tax-advantaged accounts like 401(k)s, IRAs, and Health Savings Accounts (HSAs). Contributions to these accounts are often tax-deductible, reducing your taxable income. Additionally, earnings within these accounts grow tax-free or tax deferred.

- Roth Accounts: Consider Roth IRA and Roth 401(k) accounts. While contributions are not tax-deductible, qualified withdrawals, including earnings, are tax-free. Roth accounts are particularly beneficial if you expect your tax bracket to be higher in retirement.

Tax-Efficient Investment Choices:
- Tax-Efficient Funds: Invest in tax-efficient mutual funds or exchange-traded funds (ETFs). These funds are designed to minimize taxable distributions, reducing your tax burden. Index funds are often tax-efficient due to their low turnover.
- Tax-Loss Harvesting: Implement tax-loss harvesting strategies. Sell investments that are at a loss to offset gains in other investments. This technique can reduce capital gains taxes, enhancing your after-tax returns.

Estate Planning and Tax Implications:
- Estate Tax: Understand the estate tax threshold and plan your estate accordingly. Consult with an estate planning attorney to minimize estate taxes, ensuring your heirs receive more of your assets.
- Gifting Strategies: Utilize the annual gift tax exclusion to gift assets to your heirs tax-free. Strategic gifting can reduce the value of your estate, lowering potential estate taxes.

Consulting Financial Advisors and Tax Professionals:
- Professional Guidance: Consider consulting financial advisors and tax professionals. Their expertise can help you make informed decisions regarding tax-efficient investments, estate planning, and overall financial strategies. A professional can provide personalized advice tailored to your financial situation and goals.

Conclusion: Maximizing Your Wealth
Understanding tax efficiency is like adding an extra layer of armor to your financial plan. By optimizing your investments, deductions, and credits, you minimize your tax burden, allowing more of your wealth to work for you. Strategic tax planning not only saves you money but also ensures that your hard-earned assets are preserved for your benefit and the benefit of future generations. As you move forward, remember that every dollar saved in taxes is a dollar that can contribute to your passive income streams, accelerating your journey toward financial freedom.

CHAPTER 3:
EXPLORING PASSIVE INCOME STREAMS

Introduction: Diversifying Your Income Portfolio

In this chapter, we will explore a diverse array of passive income streams, each offering unique opportunities for financial growth. From online ventures to real estate investments, this chapter serves as your guide to understanding, evaluating, and choosing the most suitable passive income streams. By the end of this chapter, you'll have the knowledge to begin building your diversified passive income portfolio.

3.1 Leveraging the Power of Online Businesses:

- Blogging and Content Creation: Learn how to monetize your passion for writing through blogging and content creation. Discover strategies for building a loyal audience and earning revenue through ads, sponsored content, and affiliate marketing.
- E-commerce and Dropshipping: Explore the world of online retail through e-commerce and dropshipping. Understand the fundamentals of setting up an online store, sourcing products, and leveraging third-party logistics for a hands-off approach to sales.
- Affiliate Marketing: Delve into the intricacies of affiliate marketing. Learn how to promote products and earn commissions for every sale made through your referral links. Master the art of selecting profitable affiliate programs and effective promotion techniques.

3.2 Real Estate Investments:

- Rental Properties: Explore the lucrative realm of rental properties. Understand the process of property acquisition, tenant management, and maximizing rental income. Learn about real estate market analysis and how to identify properties with high rental potential.
- Real Estate Crowdfunding: Discover the concept of real estate crowdfunding, allowing you to invest in properties without the hassle of property management. Learn about different crowdfunding platforms and how to assess the potential of real estate crowdfunding projects.

3.3 Stock Market and Dividend Investments:
- Dividend Stocks: Understand the power of dividend investing. Learn how to select dividend-paying stocks, create a diversified portfolio, and benefit from regular passive income in the form of dividends.
- Index Funds and ETFs: Explore the simplicity and effectiveness of index funds and exchange-traded funds (ETFs). Learn about their low fees, broad market exposure, and how they offer a hands-off approach to stock market investments.

3.4 Creating and Selling Digital Products:
- E-books and Online Courses: Leverage your expertise by creating and selling e-books and online courses. Understand the platforms for publishing and selling digital products. Learn marketing strategies to reach your target audience effectively.
- Printables and Templates: Explore the market for printables and templates. Discover how to create designs for planners, resumes, and other customizable templates. Learn about online platforms for selling digital downloads and automating the sales process.

3.5 Passive Income through Investments:
- Peer-to-Peer Lending: Understand the concept of peer-to-peer lending platforms. Learn about the risks and rewards of lending money to individuals or small businesses and earning interest in return.
- Cryptocurrency Investments: Explore the world of cryptocurrencies as a passive income opportunity. Understand the basics of blockchain technology, how to invest in cryptocurrencies, and the strategies for managing the volatile market.

Conclusion: Building Your Passive Income Empire
By exploring these diverse passive income streams, you gain insight into the vast array of opportunities available in the modern financial landscape. Each section provides actionable strategies, real-life examples, and expert tips to help you make informed decisions. As you navigate these possibilities, consider your skills, interests, and risk tolerance. Building a diversified passive income portfolio requires careful planning and continuous learning. With the knowledge gained from this chapter, you're well-equipped to embark on your passive income journey and take the next steps toward financial freedom and prosperity.

3.1 LEVERAGING THE POWER OF ONLINE BUSINESSES:

In the digital age, online businesses offer unparalleled opportunities for generating passive income. With the right strategies and dedication, you can turn your passion or expertise into a profitable venture. This section explores various online business models, providing insights into how to monetize your skills and creativity effectively.

Blogging and Content Creation:

- Finding Your Niche: Discover your passion or expertise and choose a niche for your blog. Whether it's travel, personal finance, lifestyle, or any other topic, a specific niche helps you target a dedicated audience.
- Quality Content Creation: Learn the art of creating engaging and valuable content. Understand the importance of SEO (Search Engine Optimization) to enhance your blog's visibility on search engines. Quality content attracts readers and keeps them coming back.
- Monetization Strategies: Explore different monetization methods, including:
- Ads: Earn revenue through ad networks like Google AdSense.
- Sponsored Content: Partner with brands for sponsored posts related to your niche.
- Affiliate Marketing: Promote products and earn commissions for every sale made through your referral links.
- Subscription Models: Offer premium content or memberships for exclusive access.

E-commerce and Dropshipping:

- Choosing Products: Select a niche or products you're passionate about. Research market demand and trends to identify profitable products to sell.
- Setting Up an Online Store: Use e-commerce platforms like Shopify, WooCommerce, or BigCommerce to create your online store. Customize your store's design and user experience to enhance customer satisfaction.
- Dropshipping: Explore the dropshipping model, where you sell products without handling inventory. When a customer makes a purchase, the product is shipped directly from the supplier to the customer.
Affiliate Marketing:
- Choosing the Right Products: Select affiliate products relevant to your audience and niche. Research products with high commissions and good reputations.

- Content Integration: Integrate affiliate products naturally into your content. Write genuine reviews or create tutorials that incorporate the products in a helpful way.
- Building Trust: Build trust with your audience by being transparent about your affiliate relationships. Honest recommendations lead to higher conversion rates.

Conclusion: Empowering Your Online Entrepreneurship
Leveraging the power of online businesses requires a combination of creativity, strategy, and dedication. Whether you're a blogger, an e-commerce entrepreneur, or an affiliate marketer, the key lies in providing value to your audience. Focus on creating high-quality content, understanding your audience's needs, and adapting to market trends.

By mastering these online business models, you can establish multiple streams of passive income. Keep experimenting, stay updated with industry trends, and never underestimate the potential of your creativity and determination. As you navigate the online business landscape, you're not just building a source of income; you're creating a brand and a community. Your journey to financial independence starts with your first online venture. Embrace the challenges, celebrate your successes, and continue evolving as an online entrepreneur. Your online empire awaits.

3.2 REAL ESTATE INVESTMENTS:

Real estate investments have long been a cornerstone of wealth creation. The ability to generate passive income through properties offers a tangible and potentially lucrative avenue for investors. In this section, we will explore different facets of real estate investments, from rental properties to innovative crowdfunding platforms.

Rental Properties:
- Property Selection: Carefully research and select properties based on location, potential rental income, and future market trends. Consider factors like proximity to amenities, schools, and public transportation.
- Property Management: Decide whether to manage the property yourself or hire a property management company. Property managers handle tasks like tenant screening, rent collection, and property maintenance, allowing for a more hands-off approach.
- Tenant Relations: Foster positive relationships with tenants. Promptly address concerns, conduct regular property inspections, and maintain open communication to ensure tenant satisfaction and retention.

Real Estate Crowdfunding:

- Understanding Crowdfunding Platforms: Explore real estate crowdfunding platforms that allow multiple investors to pool their resources for larger, potentially higher-yield properties. Research platforms, their fees, and the types of projects they offer.
- Diversification: Diversify your investments by participating in multiple crowdfunding projects. Spread your investments across different types of properties and locations to minimize risks associated with a specific market.
- Due Diligence: Conduct thorough due diligence on crowdfunding projects. Analyze the project's financials, the developer's track record, and the platform's terms and conditions. Understand the potential risks and rewards before investing.

Real Estate Investment Trusts (REITs):

- Understanding REITs: Real Estate Investment Trusts (REITs) are companies that own, operate, or finance income-producing real estate across various sectors. Invest in REITs to gain exposure to real estate without the need for direct property ownership.
- Types of REITs: Explore different types of REITs, including equity REITs (own and manage income-producing properties), mortgage REITs (lend money to property owners and operators), and hybrid REITs (combination of equity and mortgage REITs).
- Dividends and Tax Benefits: REITs are required to distribute at least 90% of their taxable income to shareholders in the form of dividends. Investors can benefit from regular dividend income and potential tax advantages.

Conclusion: Building Wealth through Real Estate

Real estate investments provide a tangible and potentially lucrative path to passive income. Whether you choose traditional rental properties, real estate crowdfunding, or REITs, understanding the market, conducting thorough research, and managing your investments wisely are key to success. Real estate offers not only a source of passive income but also the potential for property appreciation over time. By incorporating real estate into your investment portfolio, you're not just building passive income; you're creating a foundation for long-term wealth and financial security. As you embark on your real estate investment journey, approach each opportunity with caution, curiosity, and a long-term perspective. Your path to financial prosperity starts with your first real estate investment.

3.3 STOCK MARKET
AND DIVIDEND INVESTMENTS:

Investing in the stock market offers a wide array of opportunities for generating passive income and building long-term wealth. This section explores the strategies behind stock market investments, focusing on dividend-paying stocks, index funds, and exchange-traded funds (ETFs).

Dividend Stocks:
- Steady Income Stream: Dividend-paying stocks provide a reliable income stream. Companies that consistently pay dividends often have stable earnings and a strong financial position. Look for companies with a history of increasing dividends over time.
- Dividend Reinvestment Plans (DRIPs): Enroll in DRIPs to reinvest your dividends automatically. Reinvesting dividends allows you to buy more shares without incurring additional trading fees, enhancing your compounding returns over the long term.
- Diversification: Diversify your dividend stock portfolio across different sectors and industries. Avoid putting all your investments in a single sector to spread risk. Consider both domestic and international dividend-paying stocks for a globally diversified approach.

Index Funds and ETFs:
- Low Fees and Diversification: Index funds and ETFs offer low management fees and provide instant diversification across a specific index, sector, or asset class. Invest in broad-market index funds for overall market exposure or sector-specific ETFs for targeted investments.
- Passive Management: These funds are passively managed, meaning they aim to replicate the performance of a specific index. Passive management often results in lower fees compared to actively managed funds.
- Regular Contributions: Consider setting up automated contributions to index funds or ETFs. Regular contributions, especially when automated, allow you to benefit from dollar-cost averaging, reducing the impact of market volatility on your investments.

Reinvesting Dividends and Compounding:
- Harnessing the Power of Compounding: Reinvesting dividends is a powerful strategy for wealth accumulation. Compounding allows your invested money to grow exponentially over time, as you earn returns not just on your initial investment but also on the accumulated dividends.

- Long-Term Perspective: Adopt a long-term perspective when investing in dividend stocks, index funds, or ETFs. Market fluctuations are natural, but historically, the stock market has shown consistent growth over extended periods. Avoid reacting to short-term market movements and focus on your long-term goals.

Conclusion: Building Wealth Through Smart Stock Market Investments

Stock market investments, especially in dividend-paying stocks, index funds, and ETFs, offer a reliable path to passive income and wealth creation. By harnessing the power of compounding, diversifying your investments, and maintaining a long-term perspective, you can build a strong financial foundation. Regularly review your portfolio, stay informed about market trends, and consider consulting with a financial advisor to optimize your investment strategy. With patience, discipline, and prudent decision-making, your stock market investments can provide a steady income stream and contribute significantly to your passive income goals. As you navigate the complexities of the stock market, remember that a well-informed investor is a confident investor. Your journey toward financial prosperity begins with smart and strategic stock market investments.

3.4 CREATING AND SELLING DIGITAL PRODUCTS:

In the digital age, creating and selling digital products has become a popular and lucrative way to generate passive income. Whether you're an expert in a specific field, a creative artist, or a skilled designer, there are various digital products you can create and sell. This section explores the process of creating and marketing digital products, from e-books to online courses.

E-books and Online Courses:
• Identifying Your Expertise: Determine your areas of expertise or interests. What knowledge or skills can you share with others? E-books and online courses are excellent mediums for sharing specialized knowledge.
- Creating Engaging Content: Invest time in creating high-quality content. For e-books, focus on thorough research, engaging writing, and professional formatting. For online courses, design interactive lessons, include multimedia elements, and create quizzes or assignments for student engagement.
- Choosing the Right Platform: Select platforms for publishing and selling your digital products. Websites like Amazon Kindle Direct Publishing, Udemy, or Teachable provide user-friendly interfaces for authors and course creators. Evaluate their fees, reach, and marketing support before choosing.

Printables and Templates:
• Designing Printables: Create printable templates for various purposes, such as planners, calendars, budgeting sheets, or artistic designs. Graphic design software or online tools can help you create visually appealing printables.
• Setting Up an Online Store: Utilize platforms like Etsy or Gumroad to set up your online store. These platforms cater to creators and artists, allowing you to showcase and sell your printables to a wide audience.
• Marketing and Promotion: Use social media, blogs, or YouTube channels to market your printables. Create visually appealing previews and offer free samples to attract potential buyers. Customer reviews and testimonials can enhance your credibility.

Automating Sales and Delivery:
• Payment Gateways: Set up reliable payment gateways like PayPal or Stripe to facilitate secure transactions. Ensure your customers have multiple payment options, enhancing the convenience of the purchasing process.
• Automated Delivery: Implement automated delivery systems. Upon purchase, customers should receive instant access to downloadable files or course materials. Automation ensures a seamless experience for buyers.

Continuous Improvement and Customer Feedback:
• Feedback Loop: Encourage customer feedback. Reviews and suggestions can provide valuable insights into the quality of your products. Use this feedback to make necessary improvements and updates to your digital offerings.
• Regular Updates: Stay updated with market trends and customer preferences. Regularly update your digital products, adding new content or improving existing materials. Keeping your products fresh can attract repeat customers.

Conclusion: Monetizing Your Creativity and Knowledge
Creating and selling digital products empowers you to monetize your creativity, skills, and knowledge. By identifying your expertise, creating engaging content, and leveraging online platforms, you can build a sustainable passive income stream. The digital marketplace offers endless possibilities, whether you're an author, artist, educator, or entrepreneur. As you embark on your digital product journey, remember that quality, customer satisfaction, and continuous innovation are key to long-term success. Your digital creations not only generate income but also impact and enrich the lives of your customers. With dedication and creativity, you can turn your passion into profit and contribute meaningfully to the digital economy.

3.5 PASSIVE INCOME
THROUGH INVESTMENTS:

Investing in various financial instruments allows you to grow your wealth and generate passive income streams. This section explores two unique investment opportunities: Peer-to-Peer Lending and Cryptocurrency Investments.

Peer-to-Peer Lending:

- Understanding P2P Platforms: Peer-to-Peer lending platforms connect individual investors with borrowers. By participating, you act as a lender and earn interest on the money you lend out to individuals or small businesses.
- Diversifying Your Portfolio: Spread your investments across multiple borrowers to diversify risk. P2P platforms often allow you to invest small amounts in numerous loans, reducing the impact of defaults on your overall earnings.
- Risk Assessment: Evaluate borrowers' profiles and creditworthiness. Many P2P platforms provide credit scores and loan purposes, helping you make informed decisions. Balancing potential returns with borrower risk is crucial.

Cryptocurrency Investments:

- Understanding Cryptocurrencies: Cryptocurrencies, such as Bitcoin, Ethereum, and numerous altcoins, operate on decentralized networks using blockchain technology. They offer the potential for high returns but come with significant volatility.
- Research and Due Diligence: Thoroughly research cryptocurrencies before investing. Understand the technology, the team behind the project, market demand, and the problem the cryptocurrency aims to solve. Stay updated with news and developments in the crypto space.
- Risk Management: Only invest what you can afford to lose. Cryptocurrency investments can be highly volatile, and prices can fluctuate dramatically. Consider diversifying your investments across multiple cryptocurrencies to spread risk.

Staying Informed and Adapting:

- Continuous Learning: Cryptocurrency markets and P2P lending platforms are constantly evolving. Stay informed about changes in regulations, market trends, and technological advancements. Continuous learning is key to successful investing.
- Adaptation and Strategy: Be adaptable in your investment strategy. Market conditions can change rapidly, and your approach may need adjustment. Consider consulting with financial advisors or experts in these fields to refine your investment strategy.

Conclusion: Building Passive Income Through Strategic Investments

Investing in Peer-to-Peer lending and cryptocurrencies offers unique opportunities for generating passive income. However, they come with inherent risks that require careful consideration and strategic planning. By diversifying your investments, conducting thorough research, and staying informed, you can harness the potential of these investment avenues.

Remember, these investments require a balanced approach. While the allure of high returns is compelling, it's essential to balance potential gains with the risks involved. By adopting a cautious and informed investment strategy, you can potentially benefit from the growing world of cryptocurrencies and Peer-to-Peer lending, contributing to your overall passive income goals. Stay vigilant, stay informed, and let your investments work for you in your pursuit of financial freedom.

CHAPTER 4:
MAXIMIZING PASSIVE INCOME: STRATEGIES AND TACTICS

Introduction: The Path to Financial Freedom
In this chapter, we delve into advanced strategies and tactics to maximize your passive income potential. Here, we explore innovative ideas, tax optimization, and ways to scale existing passive income streams. By mastering the techniques outlined in this chapter, you can accelerate your journey toward financial freedom and create a legacy of wealth for future generations.

4.1 Scaling Your Passive Income Ventures:
• Leveraging Automation: Implement automation tools and systems to streamline your passive income businesses. From email marketing to customer support, automation frees up your time and allows you to scale your operations efficiently.
• Outsourcing and Delegation: Delegate tasks to freelancers or virtual assistants. Outsourcing allows you to focus on strategic aspects of your business, leading to expansion and increased profits.

4.2 Creating Membership Sites and Subscription Models:
• Building Membership Platforms: Explore the concept of membership sites where users pay a subscription fee for exclusive content or services. Learn how to create engaging membership platforms that offer value to subscribers.
• Subscription Box Services: Dive into the world of subscription box services. From niche products to curated experiences, subscription boxes provide a recurring revenue model. Understand the logistics, marketing, and customer retention strategies.

4.3 Intellectual Property and Licensing:
• Monetizing Intellectual Property: Explore licensing opportunities for your intellectual property, including patents, trademarks, and copyrights. Licensing agreements can provide royalties, turning your creations into a continuous income stream.
• Writing and Publishing Books: Learn about the world of traditional publishing versus self-publishing. Discover how to negotiate book deals, market your books, and turn your writing skills into a passive income source.

4.4 Tax Optimization Strategies:

- Understanding Tax Shelters: Explore legal tax shelters and strategies to minimize tax liabilities on your passive income. Understand the benefits of retirement accounts, real estate depreciation, and tax-efficient investments.
- Tax-Efficient Withdrawal Strategies: Plan your withdrawals strategically during retirement. Learn about the tax implications of different retirement accounts and create a withdrawal strategy that optimizes your tax situation.

4.5 Building and Selling Online Businesses:

- Flipping Websites and Online Businesses: Understand the art of website flipping. Learn how to identify undervalued online businesses, improve their value, and sell them for a profit. Explore platforms for buying and selling digital assets.
- Exit Strategies: Delve into exit strategies for online businesses. Whether it's selling to a competitor, merging, or going public, understanding exit options is crucial for maximizing your profits and ensuring a smooth transition.

Conclusion: Mastering the Art of Passive Income

By exploring advanced strategies, optimizing your tax situation, and diversifying your passive income streams, you have the potential to create a robust financial future. This chapter equips you with the knowledge and tools necessary to elevate your passive income ventures to new heights. Remember, continuous learning, adaptability, and strategic planning are the keys to mastering the art of passive income. As you implement these advanced tactics, you're not just building income streams; you're constructing a legacy of financial security and prosperity for yourself and generations to come. With dedication and strategic execution, your path to financial freedom becomes clearer, smoother, and more attainable. Let the strategies in this chapter guide you toward the life you've always dreamed of—one filled with financial independence and the freedom to live life on your terms.

4.1 SCALING YOUR PASSIVE
INCOME VENTURES:

Scaling your passive income ventures is essential for increasing your earnings without proportional increases in effort. This section explores advanced strategies to help you automate, delegate, and expand your passive income businesses.

Leveraging Automation:

- Email Marketing Automation: Implement email marketing automation tools to send targeted messages to your subscribers. Create drip campaigns, segment your audience, and personalize content, ensuring your audience receives tailored communication without constant manual intervention.
- Social Media Scheduling: Utilize social media management platforms to schedule posts across various social networks. Plan your content calendar in advance, ensuring consistent online presence without the need for real-time updates.
- Sales Funnel Automation: Design and optimize sales funnels that guide potential customers through a series of steps, leading to a purchase. Use automation tools to track customer interactions, deliver content, and initiate follow-ups, increasing your conversion rates.

Outsourcing and Delegation:

- Identifying Tasks: List tasks that can be outsourced, such as customer support, content creation, or administrative work. Identify your strengths and delegate tasks that align with others' expertise.
- Freelancer Platforms: Utilize freelancer platforms like Upwork, Fiverr, or Freelancer.com to find skilled professionals for specific tasks. Look for experienced freelancers with positive reviews to ensure quality work.
- Virtual Assistants: Hire virtual assistants to handle administrative tasks, manage schedules, or respond to customer inquiries. Virtual assistants can be a cost-effective solution for tasks that don't require physical presence.

Monitoring and Optimization:

- Data Analytics: Use analytics tools to monitor user behavior, website traffic, and sales patterns. Analyze this data to identify trends, customer preferences, and areas for improvement. Data-driven decisions can significantly optimize your passive income strategies.
- Split Testing: Implement split testing (A/B testing) for your marketing campaigns. Test different elements such as headlines, call-to-action buttons, or email subject lines to determine what resonates best with your audience. Continuous optimization enhances your conversion rates.

Strategic Partnerships:

- Affiliate Partnerships: Form partnerships with affiliates who can promote your products or services. Offer competitive commissions to motivate affiliates to drive sales. Affiliate marketing expands your reach without additional marketing expenses.
- Joint Ventures: Collaborate with other entrepreneurs or businesses in your niche for joint ventures. Pool resources, share audiences, and create mutually beneficial products or services. Joint ventures amplify your market presence and lead to potential revenue growth.

Conclusion: Scaling for Sustainable Growth

Scaling your passive income ventures requires a strategic approach. By leveraging automation, outsourcing tasks, analyzing data, and forming strategic partnerships, you can amplify your passive income streams. Continuously monitor your strategies, adapt to market changes, and focus on delivering exceptional value to your audience. With these scalable approaches, you're not just increasing your income; you're building a sustainable and thriving passive income empire. Stay innovative, stay customer-focused, and watch your ventures reach new heights of success.

4.2 CREATING MEMBERSHIP SITES AND SUBSCRIPTION MODELS:

Creating membership sites and subscription models is a powerful way to establish consistent and recurring passive income. This section explores the intricacies of building and managing subscription-based platforms, providing valuable insights into both membership sites and subscription box services.

Building Membership Platforms:
- Defining Exclusive Content: Determine the unique content or services that will be exclusive to your members. It could be premium articles, webinars, tutorials, or community forums. The value you provide will directly influence your member retention rates.
- Choosing a Platform: Select a reliable membership platform like MemberPress, Teachable, or Kajabi. Evaluate features such as payment gateways, content protection, and member communication tools. The platform should align with your specific content and audience needs.
- Community Engagement: Foster a sense of community among your members. Create forums, discussion groups, or live Q&A sessions. Member interaction not only enhances their experience but also encourages them to stay subscribed.

Subscription Box Services:
- Niche Selection: Choose a specific niche for your subscription box service. Whether it's beauty products, snacks, books, or pet supplies, a focused niche allows you to target a specific audience effectively.
- Sourcing Products: Establish relationships with suppliers and manufacturers. Negotiate bulk deals to ensure competitive pricing for your products. Quality and variety are key factors that influence subscriber satisfaction.
- Curated Experiences: Curate unique and delightful experiences for your subscribers. Personalize boxes based on individual preferences whenever possible. Consider thematic approaches for different months to keep the offerings exciting and fresh.

Pricing Strategies:
- Tiered Subscriptions: Offer different subscription tiers with varying benefits. Higher-priced tiers could include additional exclusive content, early access to products, or personalized consultations. Tiered subscriptions cater to diverse customer needs and budgets.

- Trial Periods and Discounts: Provide trial periods or discounts for new subscribers. A taste of your offerings at a reduced cost can entice potential customers to commit to a long-term subscription.

Marketing and Retention:
- Content Marketing: Create engaging content related to your subscription offerings. Blogs, videos, or social media posts that highlight the value of your products can attract new subscribers and retain existing ones.
- Retention Strategies: Implement retention strategies such as loyalty programs, referral discounts, or member-only events. Encourage long-term commitments by rewarding loyalty and ensuring subscribers feel appreciated.

Conclusion: Building Lasting Relationships with Subscribers
Creating membership sites and subscription box services is not just about providing products; it's about building a community and nurturing lasting relationships with your subscribers. By offering exclusive, valuable content or curated experiences, and by focusing on customer engagement and retention, you can establish a thriving subscription-based business. The key lies in understanding your audience, continuously innovating, and delivering exceptional value. As you cultivate your community of subscribers, you're not just earning passive income; you're creating a loyal customer base that appreciates and eagerly anticipates your offerings month after month. Stay customer-focused, stay creative, and watch your subscription-based venture flourish.

4.3 INTELLECTUAL PROPERTY AND LICENSING:

Intellectual property (IP) presents a unique avenue for generating passive income. From patents to copyrights, your creative and innovative ideas can become valuable assets. This section explores how you can monetize your intellectual property through licensing and writing and publishing books.

Monetizing Intellectual Property:
- Understanding IP Rights: Familiarize yourself with different forms of intellectual property rights, including patents, trademarks, copyrights, and trade secrets. Each type of IP protects specific aspects of your creations, inventions, or branding.

- Licensing Agreements: Enter into licensing agreements where you permit others to use your IP in exchange for royalties or fees. Licensing can apply to inventions, software, artistic creations, or even brand names. Negotiate the terms carefully to ensure fair compensation for your intellectual assets.

Writing and Publishing Books:
- Choosing Your Genre: Determine the genre or niche for your book. Whether it's fiction, non-fiction, self-help, or technical, select a genre that aligns with your expertise or passion. Research the market to identify trends and audience preferences.
- Self-Publishing vs. Traditional Publishing: Decide whether to self-publish or pursue traditional publishing. Self-publishing offers more control and higher royalties, while traditional publishing provides access to wider distribution networks and professional support. Evaluate which option suits your goals and resources.
- Marketing and Promotion: Invest in book marketing strategies. Utilize social media, author websites, book signings, and virtual events to create buzz around your book. Positive reviews, engaging book covers, and compelling book descriptions are crucial for attracting readers.

E-books, Audiobooks, and Print-on-Demand:
- E-books and Audiobooks: Expand your reach by publishing e-book and audiobook versions of your work. E-books are accessible on various platforms, while audiobooks cater to auditory learners. Offering multiple formats enhances your book's appeal.
- Print-on-Demand Services: Utilize print-on-demand services like Amazon's KDP Print or IngramSpark. Print-on-demand allows you to offer paperback versions of your book without maintaining inventory. When a book is ordered, it's printed and shipped, eliminating upfront costs.

Conclusion: Transforming Creativity into Profitable Ventures
Monetizing intellectual property and publishing books empower you to transform your creativity and knowledge into profitable ventures. Licensing agreements allow you to earn royalties from your inventions or creations, while writing and publishing books enable you to share your expertise with a global audience. By understanding the market, selecting the right publishing methods, and effectively marketing your creations, you can generate passive income while leaving a lasting impact on readers and users alike.

As you embark on these ventures, remember that intellectual property is not just a legal concept; it's a valuable asset that can fuel your financial success for years to come. Stay innovative, stay persistent, and let your creativity shine as you turn your ideas into revenue-generating intellectual properties.

4.4 TAX OPTIMIZATION STRATEGIES:

Optimizing your taxes is a crucial aspect of maximizing your passive income. This section explores various tax optimization strategies to minimize your tax liabilities and increase your overall earnings.

Understanding Tax Shelters:

- Retirement Accounts: Contribute to tax-advantaged retirement accounts such as 401(k)s, IRAs, or Roth IRAs. These accounts offer tax benefits, allowing your investments to grow tax-free or tax-deferred, depending on the account type.
- Real Estate Depreciation: If you own rental properties, take advantage of depreciation deductions. The IRS allows you to deduct a portion of the property's value each year, reducing your taxable income.
- Tax-Efficient Investments: Invest in tax-efficient funds, index funds, or ETFs. These investments typically generate fewer taxable events, resulting in lower capital gains taxes.

Tax-Efficient Withdrawal Strategies:

- Roth IRA Conversions: Consider converting traditional IRA funds to Roth IRAs, especially during years with lower income. Roth IRAs allow tax-free withdrawals in retirement, providing tax diversification in your retirement income.
- Tax-Loss Harvesting: Implement tax-loss harvesting by selling losing investments to offset gains in your portfolio. This strategy can help minimize your capital gains taxes.
- Qualified Dividends and Capital Gains: Take advantage of lower tax rates on qualified dividends and long-term capital gains. Holding investments for more than a year qualifies them for these favorable tax rates.

Business Expenses and Deductions:

• Home Office Deduction: If you run a business from home, you may be eligible for a home office deduction. Calculate the portion of your home used for business purposes and deduct related expenses like utilities and mortgage interest.

- Business Expenses: Keep detailed records of business-related expenses. Deductible expenses may include office supplies, marketing costs, professional fees, and travel expenses. Proper documentation is essential to claim these deductions.

Hiring a Tax Professional:
- Tax Advisor Consultation: Consider consulting a tax professional or advisor specializing in your type of income. They can provide personalized advice tailored to your financial situation, ensuring you take advantage of all available tax-saving opportunities.
- Regular Tax Planning: Engage in regular tax planning sessions, especially before the end of the fiscal year. Proactive tax planning can help you make strategic financial decisions to minimize your tax liabilities.

Conclusion: Keeping More of Your Earnings
Tax optimization is not about evading taxes but about utilizing legal strategies to keep more of your hard-earned money. By understanding the nuances of tax shelters, efficient withdrawal methods, business deductions, and seeking professional advice, you can significantly reduce your tax burden. The money saved in taxes can be reinvested, further growing your passive income streams. Stay informed, stay organized, and make tax optimization an integral part of your overall financial strategy. With careful planning and adherence to tax laws, you can maximize your passive income while legally minimizing your tax obligations, ultimately securing a more prosperous financial future.

4.5 BUILDING AND SELLING ONLINE BUSINESSES:

Building and selling online businesses can be a lucrative strategy for generating substantial profits and realizing significant returns on your investments. This section explores the process of building online ventures and outlines effective exit strategies for selling them at a profit.

Flipping Websites and Online Businesses:
- Identifying Profitable Niches: Research trending and profitable niches in the online space. Look for opportunities where you can add value or innovate within a specific market. Niches with high demand and growth potential often attract buyers.

- Building Valuable Assets: Develop your online business into a valuable asset. Focus on creating high-quality content, building a strong brand, optimizing user experience, and implementing effective marketing strategies. A well-maintained and profitable online business attracts potential buyers.

Exit Strategies:
- Selling to Competitors: Explore the option of selling your business to competitors within your niche. Competitors may be interested in acquiring your customer base, technology, or market share. Negotiate strategically to obtain the best deal.
- Merging with Similar Businesses: Consider merging your business with a similar venture. Mergers can create synergies, reduce competition, and enhance the overall value proposition. Collaborate with businesses that complement your offerings.

Selling on Online Marketplaces:
- Platforms like Flippa: Utilize online marketplaces like Flippa to list and sell your online business. Provide comprehensive details about your business, including revenue, traffic statistics, and growth potential. Quality listings attract serious buyers willing to pay a premium for established businesses.
- Preparing Due Diligence Documents: Prepare due diligence documents showcasing the financial health, growth trajectory, customer base, and operational processes of your business. Transparent and well-documented information builds buyer confidence.

Negotiation and Transfer:
- Effective Negotiation: Negotiate the terms of the sale effectively. Be clear about your expectations and seek professional advice if necessary. Address concerns, provide clarifications, and work towards a mutually beneficial agreement.
- Smooth Transition: Facilitate a smooth transition for the new owner. Provide necessary training, transfer domain names and hosting accounts, and introduce the buyer to key stakeholders. A seamless transition enhances the business's long-term success.

Conclusion: Profits in Business Transactions

Building and selling online businesses can be a highly profitable venture. By identifying lucrative niches, creating valuable assets, exploring various exit strategies, and mastering the art of negotiation, you can realize substantial profits. Whether you're a serial entrepreneur or an investor looking for profitable opportunities, the online marketplace offers a fertile ground for financial growth.

Remember, successful transactions are built on trust, transparency, and a clear understanding of market dynamics. By staying informed, leveraging professional assistance when necessary, and approaching each deal strategically, you can capitalize on the lucrative world of online business transactions. With astute decision-making and a keen eye for profitable ventures, you can turn your online businesses into valuable assets, ensuring a prosperous future in the digital economy.

CHAPTER 5:
SUSTAINING AND GROWING YOUR PASSIVE INCOME EMPIRE

Introduction: The Journey Continues
In this final chapter, we delve into strategies to sustain and grow your passive income empire over the long term. Building a robust passive income stream is just the beginning; sustaining it and ensuring its growth are essential for lasting financial success. This chapter explores methods to protect your investments, diversify your income streams, and continue building wealth.

5.1 Protecting Your Passive Income:
- Insurance and Risk Management: Explore insurance options to protect your investments, properties, and assets. From property insurance to liability coverage, safeguarding your wealth from unexpected events is crucial.
- Estate Planning: Develop a comprehensive estate plan to ensure the smooth transition of your assets to your heirs. Establish wills, trusts, and powers of attorney to protect your wealth and provide for your loved ones.

5.2 Diversifying Your Income Streams:
- Exploring New Ventures: Continuously explore new passive income opportunities. Stay updated with market trends and emerging industries. Diversifying into different sectors can spread risks and increase your overall income potential.
- Investing in Stocks, Real Estate, and Businesses: Diversify your investments across stocks, real estate properties, and businesses. Each asset class offers unique advantages and risks. A diversified portfolio can provide stability and resilience against market fluctuations.

5.3 Passive Income in Retirement:
- Retirement Income Planning: Plan for passive income during retirement. Ensure your investments provide a steady income stream to support your lifestyle without depleting your principal. Consider annuities, dividends, and interest-bearing accounts for reliable retirement income.
- Long-Term Care and Health Planning: Account for potential healthcare costs in retirement. Long-term care insurance and health savings accounts (HSAs) can protect your assets from the financial burden of medical expenses.

5.4 Sustainable and Ethical Investments:

- Impact Investing: Consider impact investing, where you invest in companies or funds that align with your ethical and social values. Impact investments support causes such as renewable energy, clean water, or social justice, allowing you to create a positive impact while earning passive income.
- Sustainable Real Estate: Explore sustainable real estate investments, such as eco-friendly properties or green energy projects. Sustainable real estate not only generates passive income but also contributes to environmental conservation.

Conclusion: The Endless Possibilities of Passive Income

As you navigate the intricacies of sustaining and growing your passive income empire, remember that the journey toward financial freedom is ongoing. By protecting your investments, diversifying your income streams, planning for retirement, and considering sustainable and ethical investments, you can ensure your wealth continues to flourish.

Passive income is not just a financial strategy; it's a mindset that empowers you to create a life of abundance and security. Embrace the endless possibilities of passive income, stay curious, and remain open to new opportunities. With a proactive approach, continuous learning, and a commitment to your financial goals, your passive income empire can evolve into a legacy of prosperity for you and future generations. As you step into the future, let the principles of passive income guide you toward a life filled with financial stability, limitless potential, and the freedom to live life on your terms.

5.1 PROTECTING
YOUR PASSIVE INCOME:

Safeguarding your passive income is crucial to ensuring its stability and longevity. This section explores essential strategies to protect your investments and assets, allowing you to weather unforeseen challenges and maintain a secure financial future.

Insurance and Risk Management:

- Property Insurance: If you own real estate properties, invest in comprehensive property insurance. This insurance covers damages to your properties caused by fire, theft, natural disasters, or vandalism, providing financial protection against unexpected events.
- Liability Insurance: Consider liability insurance to protect your assets from potential legal claims. Liability insurance can cover legal fees, settlements, or judgments if you're held responsible for someone else's injuries or damages.

Estate Planning:
- Wills and Trusts: Draft a legally binding will outlining how you want your assets to be distributed after your passing. Establish trusts, if applicable, to protect your assets from estate taxes and ensure they are managed according to your wishes.
- Power of Attorney: Designate a power of attorney, granting someone you trust the authority to make financial decisions on your behalf if you become incapacitated. This ensures that your affairs are managed efficiently, even if you are unable to do so yourself.

Emergency Funds and Liquidity:
- Emergency Fund: Maintain an emergency fund equal to at least six months' worth of living expenses. An emergency fund acts as a financial safety net, allowing you to cover unexpected expenses or losses of income without disrupting your passive income streams.
- Liquidity Planning: Ensure you have liquid assets readily available. Liquidity provides you with the flexibility to seize investment opportunities, cover emergencies, or adapt to changing market conditions without resorting to distress sales.

Legal Protections:
- Legal Consultation: Consult with legal professionals to understand the legal implications of your investments and passive income ventures. Proper legal structures, contracts, and agreements can protect your interests and prevent potential disputes.
- Intellectual Property Protection: If your passive income involves intellectual property, such as patents, trademarks, or copyrights, ensure they are legally protected. Enforce your intellectual property rights to prevent unauthorized use or duplication.

Conclusion: Building a Fortress for Your Wealth
Protecting your passive income is akin to building a fortress for your wealth. By investing in insurance, planning your estate, maintaining emergency funds, ensuring liquidity, and securing legal protections, you create a strong defense against financial setbacks.

Remember that proactive measures today can prevent significant losses in the future. Regularly review your insurance policies, update your wills and trusts as your circumstances change, and stay informed about legal and financial best practices. With a well-protected passive income, you can face challenges with confidence, knowing that your financial foundation is secure, resilient, and capable of withstanding unforeseen circumstances.

5.2 DIVERSIFYING YOUR INCOME STREAMS:

Diversifying your income streams is a fundamental strategy for sustaining and growing your wealth. By spreading your investments across various avenues, you mitigate risks and create a more stable and resilient financial portfolio. This section explores the importance of diversification and provides insights into effective methods of expanding your income sources.

Exploring New Ventures:
- Market Research: Continuously conduct market research to identify emerging trends and profitable opportunities. Stay updated on consumer behavior, technological advancements, and industry shifts. Exploring new ventures allows you to capitalize on evolving market demands.
- Innovation and Creativity: Foster a culture of innovation and creativity. Encourage brainstorming sessions and idea generation within your business or investment circles. Innovative solutions and unique offerings can open doors to new income streams.

Investing in Stocks, Real Estate, and Businesses:
- Stock Market Investments: Diversify your investment portfolio by investing in stocks of different sectors and industries. Consider index funds or exchange-traded funds (ETFs) to gain exposure to a broad range of stocks, spreading your risk across the market.
- Real Estate Properties: Invest in real estate properties in diverse locations. Residential, commercial, and vacation properties offer varied income streams. Rental income, property appreciation, and tax benefits contribute to the profitability of real estate investments.
- Business Ventures: Explore opportunities for investing in existing businesses or startups. Consider becoming an angel investor or venture capitalist. Investing in businesses allows you to benefit from their growth and success.

Digital Ventures and Online Platforms:
- E-commerce and Dropshipping: Explore e-commerce platforms and dropshipping models. Setting up online stores and utilizing dropshipping suppliers enable you to sell products without managing inventory. E-commerce offers vast market reach and scalability.
- Affiliate Marketing: Engage in affiliate marketing by promoting products or services from other companies.

Earn commissions for every sale made through your referral links. Affiliate marketing provides a passive income stream without the need for product creation.

Creating Passive Income Streams from Existing Skills:
- Freelancing and Consultation: Offer your skills and expertise on freelancing platforms. Provide services such as writing, graphic design, programming, or consultancy. Freelancing allows you to monetize your talents on a project basis.
- Online Courses and Workshops: Create and sell online courses or workshops based on your expertise. Platforms like Udemy, Teachable, or Skillshare provide tools to develop and market your educational content. Share your knowledge and earn passive income from course sales.

Conclusion: Building a Resilient Financial Future
Diversifying your income streams is not just a strategy; it's a mindset that ensures your financial resilience. By exploring new ventures, investing in different asset classes, embracing digital opportunities, and leveraging your skills, you create a multifaceted income portfolio.

Remember that diversification requires careful planning and assessment of risks. Regularly monitor your investments, adapt to market changes, and stay informed about the performance of your income streams. With a diversified portfolio, you not only protect your wealth but also position yourself for continuous growth and financial prosperity. As you expand your income sources, you're not just building wealth; you're forging a resilient and prosperous financial future for yourself and your loved ones. Stay innovative, stay vigilant, and let the diversity of your income streams be the cornerstone of your enduring financial success.

5.3 PASSIVE INCOME
IN RETIREMENT:

Planning for passive income during retirement is essential to maintain your financial stability and lifestyle after you stop working. This section explores strategies to ensure a steady stream of income during your retirement years, allowing you to enjoy the fruits of your labor without financial stress.

Retirement Income Planning:
- Annuities: Consider investing in annuities, which provide a series of payments made at equal intervals. Fixed annuities offer predictable income, while variable annuities allow you to invest in a range of funds, potentially yielding higher returns.

- Dividend Stocks: Build a portfolio of dividend-paying stocks. Dividend income can be a reliable source of funds during retirement. Look for stable companies with a history of consistent dividends to ensure a dependable income stream.

Real Estate Investments:
- Rental Properties: If you own rental properties, they can serve as a source of passive income during retirement. Properly managed rental properties generate regular income and, in some cases, can be adjusted for inflation through rent increases.
- Reverse Mortgages: Explore reverse mortgages as an option if you own your home. A reverse mortgage allows you to convert a portion of your home equity into cash without selling your property. This can provide a reliable income stream while allowing you to continue living in your home.

Long-Term Care and Health Planning:
- Long-Term Care Insurance: Invest in long-term care insurance to cover potential expenses related to assisted living, nursing home care, or in-home assistance. Long-term care insurance can protect your assets from the significant costs associated with extended healthcare needs.
- Health Savings Accounts (HSAs): Contribute to Health Savings Accounts during your working years. HSAs offer tax advantages, and the funds can be withdrawn tax-free for qualified medical expenses in retirement, providing a tax-efficient way to cover healthcare costs.

Passive Income from Investments:
- Dividend and Interest Income: Structure your investments to generate dividends and interest income. Focus on bonds, dividend-paying stocks, and other interest-bearing instruments. These forms of passive income can provide a steady cash flow for your living expenses.
- Income from Funds and ETFs: Invest in mutual funds or exchange-traded funds (ETFs) that focus on income-generating assets. These funds often distribute dividends and interest income, offering you a regular income stream while maintaining a diversified investment portfolio.

Conclusion: Enjoying a Comfortable Retirement
Planning for passive income in retirement is about creating financial security and peace of mind during your golden years.

By diversifying your income sources, investing in stable assets, considering insurance options, and planning for healthcare costs, you can ensure a comfortable and worry-free retirement. Regularly review your retirement plan as you approach retirement age, adjusting your strategies based on market conditions and personal needs. A well-thought-out retirement income plan allows you to enjoy your retirement years to the fullest, pursuing your passions and spending quality time with loved ones, secure in the knowledge that your financial future is well taken care of. Stay proactive, stay informed, and let your carefully planned passive income streams provide the foundation for a fulfilling and enjoyable retirement.

5.4 SUSTAINABLE AND ETHICAL INVESTMENTS:

Investing sustainably and ethically not only aligns your financial goals but also allows you to contribute positively to society and the environment. This section explores the importance of sustainable investments and ethical choices, enabling you to create a lasting impact while earning passive income.

Impact Investing:
- Environmental Conservation: Invest in projects or companies focused on environmental conservation. These initiatives can include renewable energy, clean water, sustainable agriculture, and wildlife conservation. Impact investments in these areas promote eco-friendly practices and protect natural resources.
- Social Justice Initiatives: Support businesses that prioritize social justice initiatives. Invest in companies working toward gender equality, racial diversity, or economic empowerment in underserved communities. Socially responsible investments contribute to a more equitable society.

Sustainable Real Estate:
- Green Buildings: Invest in green buildings or retrofit existing properties to meet eco-friendly standards. Green buildings are energy-efficient, environmentally friendly, and often result in reduced operational costs. Sustainable real estate investments contribute to environmental preservation while providing passive income through rentals or leases.
- Renewable Energy Projects: Explore investments in renewable energy projects such as solar farms, wind energy, or hydroelectric power. Renewable energy investments generate consistent passive income through energy sales while promoting clean energy alternatives.

Ethical Consumer Goods:
- Organic Farming: Support organic farming initiatives and invest in businesses that promote organic produce and sustainable agriculture. Organic farming not only provides healthier food options but also promotes environmentally friendly farming practices.
- Fair Trade Products: Invest in fair trade businesses that ensure fair wages and ethical treatment of workers in developing countries. Fair trade products empower local communities, alleviate poverty, and promote sustainable economic development.

Conclusion: Creating Positive Change through Investments

Sustainable and ethical investments empower you to create positive change while earning passive income. By supporting environmentally conscious initiatives, promoting social justice, and investing in ethical consumer goods, you actively contribute to a better world.

Consider integrating sustainable and ethical investments into your portfolio, aligning your financial goals with your values. Research companies and projects, evaluate their impact, and make informed decisions that resonate with your ethical principles. By investing responsibly, you not only secure your financial future but also contribute to a more sustainable and equitable world for generations to come. Stay conscious, stay engaged, and let your investments be a force for positive change.

CHAPTER 6:
NAVIGATING CHALLENGES AND EMBRACING GROWTH

Introduction: Embracing Resilience

In this chapter, we explore the challenges that come with building and maintaining passive income streams and discuss strategies to overcome them. We also delve into advanced techniques to further optimize your passive income ventures and ensure sustained growth. Embracing resilience and adaptability are key themes as we navigate the dynamic landscape of passive income generation.

6.1 Overcoming Common Challenges:

- Market Volatility: Learn how to weather market fluctuations and adapt your strategies to changing economic conditions. Diversification, strategic planning, and a long-term perspective can mitigate the impact of market volatility on your passive income.
- Regulatory Changes: Stay informed about legal and regulatory changes that may affect your passive income ventures. Proactive compliance and adapting your business model to new regulations are essential to avoid legal challenges and disruptions.
- Technological Advancements: Embrace technology and automation to optimize your passive income streams. Leverage emerging tools and platforms to streamline operations, reach wider audiences, and enhance customer experiences.

6.2 Advanced Strategies for Optimization:

- Data-Driven Decision Making: Utilize data analytics to gain insights into customer behavior, market trends, and the performance of your income streams. Data-driven decisions can refine your strategies, enhance user engagement, and increase conversion rates.
- Scaling Through Outsourcing: Explore outsourcing options to delegate non-core tasks. By outsourcing routine activities, you can focus on strategic aspects of your business, allowing for scalability and efficient use of resources.
- Continuous Innovation: Foster a culture of innovation within your passive income ventures. Stay ahead of the competition by continuously updating your products, services, or content. Innovation keeps your offerings fresh and appealing to your audience.

6.3 Building Passive Income Portfolios:

- Balancing Risk and Reward: Diversify your passive income portfolio with a mix of low-risk and higher-yield investments. Evaluate risk tolerance and adjust your portfolio accordingly. Balance stable, long-term investments with higher-risk, potentially higher-reward opportunities.
- Staying Adaptable: Embrace adaptability as a core principle. Markets change, consumer preferences evolve, and new opportunities emerge. Being adaptable allows you to pivot when necessary, ensuring your passive income ventures remain relevant and profitable.

6.4 Cultivating a Growth Mindset:

- Continuous Learning: Invest in your knowledge and skills. Stay updated with industry trends, attend workshops, read books, and participate in online courses. Continuous learning enhances your expertise and equips you to make informed decisions.
- Embracing Failure: Understand that failures are valuable learning experiences. Embrace setbacks as opportunities to refine your strategies, innovate, and grow. A growth mindset allows you to bounce back stronger and more resilient than before.

Conclusion: Mastering the Art of Resilient Passive Income

Navigating challenges and embracing growth in the world of passive income requires a combination of strategic planning, adaptability, and a resilient mindset. By overcoming common challenges, optimizing your strategies, building diversified portfolios, and fostering a growth mindset, you can master the art of resilient passive income.

Remember that every challenge is an opportunity to learn and innovate. Stay proactive, remain open to change, and view setbacks as stepping stones toward greater success. With determination, continuous learning, and a commitment to adaptability, your passive income ventures can not only withstand challenges but also thrive, ensuring sustained growth and financial prosperity for years to come. Stay resilient, stay innovative, and let your passive income journey be a testament to your unwavering commitment to financial freedom and abundance.

6.1 OVERCOMING COMMON CHALLENGES:

Building and maintaining passive income streams can be a rewarding endeavor, but it comes with its share of challenges. Recognizing and proactively addressing these challenges is key to long-term success. In this section, we'll explore some of the most common challenges faced by passive income entrepreneurs and strategies to overcome them.

Market Volatility and Economic Downturns:
- Strategy Diversification: Diversify your passive income streams across different sectors and investment types. A varied portfolio can help mitigate losses during economic downturns. For instance, if one industry is affected, other investments might remain stable.
- Emergency Funds: Maintain an emergency fund to cover living expenses for at least six months. Having a financial safety net provides stability during uncertain times and allows you to continue investing without being forced to sell assets at a loss.

Regulatory Changes and Compliance Issues:
- Stay Informed: Keep abreast of regulatory changes in the areas where you operate. Regularly update your knowledge regarding tax laws, business regulations, and industry-specific compliance requirements. Engage legal and financial professionals to ensure your ventures comply with all regulations.
- Adaptability: Build a business model that can adapt to regulatory changes. Anticipate potential shifts and have contingency plans in place. Being agile and ready to pivot your strategies can minimize the impact of regulatory challenges.

Technological Advancements and Market Trends:
- Continuous Learning: Invest in ongoing education to stay current with technological advancements. Attend workshops, webinars, and conferences related to your industry. Embrace emerging technologies to enhance your products or services and remain competitive.
- Collaboration and Networking: Collaborate with tech-savvy professionals or companies. Networking with innovators can offer insights into emerging trends and technologies. Partnerships can help you leverage new tools without a steep learning curve.

Competition and Market Saturation:

- Niche Specialization: Focus on a niche market where you can excel. Specializing allows you to become an expert in a specific area, making it easier to stand out among competitors. Identify gaps in the market and tailor your offerings to address unmet needs.
- Customer Engagement: Build strong relationships with your customers. Exceptional customer service, personalized experiences, and active engagement on social media can create a loyal customer base. Satisfied customers are more likely to recommend your products or services, helping you expand your reach.

Conclusion: Proactive Strategies for Long-Term Success

Overcoming common challenges in passive income ventures requires a combination of strategic planning, adaptability, and continuous learning. By diversifying your strategies, staying informed about regulations, embracing technological advancements, and building strong customer relationships, you can navigate challenges effectively.

Remember, challenges are inherent in any business venture; it's how you respond to them that defines your success. Stay proactive, remain open to change, and view challenges as opportunities for growth and innovation. With resilience, strategic thinking, and a customer-focused approach, you can overcome obstacles and build a thriving and sustainable passive income empire. Stay determined, stay adaptable, and let your ability to overcome challenges be the driving force behind your long-term success.

6.2 ADVANCED STRATEGIES FOR OPTIMIZATION:

Once you've established your passive income streams, the journey doesn't end; it evolves. Advanced strategies are essential to optimize your existing ventures, scale your efforts, and ensure sustained growth. In this section, we delve into sophisticated techniques to enhance efficiency and maximize your passive income potential.

Data-Driven Decision Making:

- Advanced Analytics: Utilize advanced analytics tools and techniques to gain deep insights into customer behavior, market trends, and ROI. Predictive analytics can help you anticipate customer needs and tailor your offerings accordingly, enhancing customer satisfaction and increasing sales.

Scaling Through Outsourcing:
- Virtual Teams: Build virtual teams comprising skilled professionals from around the world. Leverage platforms like Upwork and Fiverr to find experts in various fields. Outsourcing tasks such as customer support, content creation, or administrative work can free up your time for strategic decision-making.
- Project Management Tools: Invest in project management tools like Asana, Trello, or Monday.com. These platforms streamline collaboration, facilitate communication, and ensure tasks are completed efficiently. Centralized project management enhances productivity, allowing you to manage multiple ventures seamlessly.

Continuous Innovation:
- Innovation Labs: Establish an innovation lab within your organization. Dedicate a team to explore emerging technologies, market trends, and customer preferences. Experiment with new ideas and concepts, fostering a culture of innovation that keeps your products or services at the forefront of your industry.
- Open Innovation: Collaborate with external partners, startups, or academic institutions through open innovation initiatives. Open innovation fosters creativity and allows you to access external expertise and ideas. Joint ventures and partnerships can lead to innovative products or services that capture new markets.

Blockchain and Smart Contracts:
- Blockchain Integration: Explore blockchain technology for your business operations. Blockchain offers transparent and secure transactions, reducing fraud and enhancing customer trust. Investigate how blockchain can optimize supply chains, payment systems, or digital rights management.
- Smart Contracts: Implement smart contracts for automated, secure, and transparent transactions. Smart contracts, powered by blockchain, streamline processes such as royalty payments, content licensing, or affiliate marketing. Automating these processes reduces administrative overhead and ensures accurate, timely transactions.

Conclusion: Elevating Your Passive Income Ventures
Advanced strategies for optimization are about elevating your passive income ventures to new heights. By harnessing the power of data-driven insights, leveraging virtual teams, fostering a culture of innovation, and exploring cutting-edge technologies like blockchain, you position your ventures for unparalleled success.

Remember, optimization is an ongoing process. Continuously assess your strategies, stay updated with industry advancements, and remain open to experimentation. With a forward-thinking approach, your passive income ventures can not only withstand market challenges but also lead the way in your industry. Embrace innovation, embrace collaboration, and let your commitment to continuous improvement drive your ventures toward extraordinary achievements. Stay visionary, stay dynamic, and let your optimized passive income ventures set new standards in the world of financial abundance and entrepreneurial excellence.

6.3 BUILDING PASSIVE INCOME PORTFOLIOS:

Building a diversified and resilient passive income portfolio is fundamental to long-term financial success. In this section, we explore advanced strategies for constructing and managing robust portfolios, ensuring stable income streams and sustained growth.

Balancing Risk and Reward:
- Risk Assessment: Conduct a thorough risk assessment for each investment. Understand the volatility, market trends, and historical performance. Allocate your investments strategically, balancing high-risk, high-reward opportunities with stable, low-risk assets. Regularly review and adjust your portfolio based on changing market conditions.
- Asset Allocation: Diversify across asset classes such as stocks, bonds, real estate, and alternative investments like cryptocurrencies or commodities. Each asset class performs differently under varying economic conditions, providing stability to your portfolio. Allocate assets based on your risk tolerance, financial goals, and time horizon.

Staying Adaptable:
- Market Monitoring: Stay vigilant about market trends and global events. Monitor economic indicators, geopolitical developments, and technological advancements. Being aware of shifts in the market allows you to adjust your portfolio in response to emerging opportunities or potential risks.
- Active Management: Consider active management of your investments, especially in sectors with rapid developments. Actively managed funds or hiring a professional financial advisor can provide expertise in optimizing your portfolio. Regularly rebalance your assets to maintain the desired allocation and risk profile.

Passive Income Investments:

- Dividend Growth Stocks: Focus on dividend growth stocks from stable companies with a history of increasing dividends. These stocks offer both passive income through dividends and the potential for capital appreciation over time. Reinvest dividends to maximize your returns.
- Real Estate Investment Trusts (REITs): Invest in REITs to gain exposure to real estate properties without the hassle of property management. REITs distribute a significant portion of their earnings to shareholders, providing a steady income stream. Research different types of REITs, including residential, commercial, and industrial, to diversify your real estate holdings.

Long-Term Investments:

- Compounding Interest: Leverage the power of compounding interest by reinvesting your earnings. Compounding allows your investments to grow exponentially over time. Reinvest dividends, interest, and capital gains to benefit from compounding, accelerating the growth of your passive income.
- Retirement Accounts: Contribute to retirement accounts like 401(k)s or IRAs. These accounts offer tax advantages, allowing your investments to grow tax-deferred or tax-free. Take advantage of employer matching contributions and explore the full range of investment options within these accounts.

Conclusion: A Secure and Thriving Future

Building passive income portfolios is a nuanced art that requires careful planning, diversification, and adaptability. By balancing risk and reward, staying adaptable to market dynamics, and investing in reliable sources of passive income, you can create a secure and thriving financial future.

Remember that building passive income portfolios is not a one-time task but an ongoing process. Regularly assess your investments, stay informed about market

trends, and remain open to adjusting your strategies. With a well-managed portfolio, you can enjoy financial stability, generate reliable passive income, and achieve your long-term financial goals. Stay diligent, stay informed, and let your thoughtfully constructed passive income portfolios pave the way for a prosperous and secure future.

6.4 CULTIVATING A
GROWTH MINDSET:

Cultivating a growth mindset is the foundation for enduring success in the realm of passive income. It's not merely about wealth accumulation but a continuous journey of learning, adapting, and evolving. In this section, we explore the transformative power of a growth mindset and how it can fuel your passive income ventures toward greater heights.

Continuous Learning:
- Embrace Curiosity: Cultivate a curious mindset that drives you to explore new ideas, industries, and investment opportunities. Read voraciously, attend seminars, and engage with thought leaders. The more you learn, the better equipped you are to identify innovative ways to generate passive income.
- Stay Tech-Savvy: Technology evolves rapidly. Stay updated with technological advancements relevant to your ventures. Understand blockchain, artificial intelligence, and other emerging technologies. Technological literacy opens doors to novel passive income avenues and keeps you competitive in the digital landscape.

Embracing Failure:
- Redefine Failure: See setbacks as valuable lessons rather than failures. Analyze what went wrong, learn from it, and apply those lessons in future endeavors. Every failure is a stepping stone toward success, offering insights that can lead to more informed decisions.
- Risk-Taking: Embrace calculated risks. Understand that not every venture will succeed, but each failure brings you closer to the right strategy. Fear of failure can paralyze progress; instead, view risks as opportunities for growth and innovation.

Adaptability and Innovation:
- Agile Decision-Making: Cultivate the ability to make swift decisions based on changing circumstances. Be adaptable and open to change. The ability to pivot your strategies in response to market dynamics is a hallmark of successful entrepreneurs.
- Innovate Continuously: Innovation should be at the core of your mindset. Encourage a culture of innovation within your teams. Experiment with new business models, products, or services. Innovation keeps your passive income ventures fresh and appealing to your audience.

Building Resilience:

- Mental and Emotional Resilience: Building passive income requires resilience. Develop mental and emotional strength to navigate challenges. Practice mindfulness, meditation, or other stress-reducing techniques. A resilient mindset helps you stay focused and optimistic even in challenging times.
- Seek Mentorship: Surround yourself with mentors and peers who inspire and challenge you. Learning from others' experiences can provide valuable insights. Mentorship accelerates your learning curve and equips you with the wisdom to make informed decisions.

Conclusion: The Infinite Potential of Growth

Cultivating a growth mindset is not just a strategy; it's a way of life. It propels you beyond the limits of your comfort zone and unleashes your infinite potential. With a growth mindset, challenges become opportunities, failures become lessons, and passive income ventures become epic journeys of continuous growth.

Embrace the unknown, welcome change, and nurture your curiosity. Your mindset is the compass that guides your passive income ventures toward unprecedented success. As you cultivate a growth mindset, you embark on a transformative journey, not just in the realm of finance but in the depths of your own capabilities. Stay hungry for knowledge, stay resilient in the face of challenges, and let your unwavering growth mindset be the beacon that lights your path to enduring wealth and fulfillment.

CHAPTER 7:
LEGACY BUILDING AND GIVING BACK

Introduction: Beyond Financial Abundance

In this concluding chapter, we shift our focus from personal wealth to the impact of passive income on society and the legacy you can leave behind. Building wealth isn't just about personal prosperity; it's an opportunity to make a difference in the lives of others and contribute to the betterment of the world. In this chapter, we explore the significance of legacy building, philanthropy, and the profound satisfaction that comes from giving back.

7.1 Creating a Lasting Legacy:

- Defining Your Legacy: Reflect on the legacy you want to leave behind. Consider the values, principles, and causes that are important to you. Your legacy can extend beyond financial contributions; it can encompass knowledge sharing, mentorship, and inspiring future generations.
- Educational Endowments: Contribute to education by establishing scholarships, endowments, or funding educational initiatives. Education is a powerful tool for societal progress. By providing access to quality education, you empower individuals to transform their lives and communities.

7.2 Philanthropy and Social Impact:

- Strategic Philanthropy: Adopt a strategic approach to philanthropy. Identify causes aligned with your values and goals. Research and support organizations making a significant impact in those areas. Strategic giving maximizes the effectiveness of your contributions.
- Social Entrepreneurship: Explore social entrepreneurship as a means of creating sustainable social impact. Support or establish businesses that address social or environmental challenges. Social entrepreneurs leverage market-driven approaches to tackle societal issues, fostering positive change and financial sustainability.

7.3 Mentorship and Knowledge Sharing:

- Mentoring Future Leaders: Share your knowledge and experiences with aspiring entrepreneurs and professionals. Mentorship accelerates personal and professional growth, empowering individuals to achieve their full potential. Your guidance can shape the leaders of tomorrow.

- Authorship and Thought Leadership: Consider writing a book, creating online courses, or sharing your expertise through public speaking. Your insights can inspire and educate others, fostering a culture of continuous learning and innovation.

7.4 Sustainability and Environmental Conservation:

- Supporting Green Initiatives: Contribute to environmental conservation efforts. Support organizations focused on reforestation, wildlife protection, or clean energy initiatives. Environmental sustainability is crucial for the well-being of future generations.
- Promoting Eco-Friendly Practices: Encourage eco-friendly practices within your community and industry. Advocate for sustainable business models, reduce waste, and promote renewable energy solutions. Small changes collectively create a significant impact on the environment.

Conclusion: A Legacy of Impact and Compassion

Building a legacy through passive income ventures is about more than financial abundance; it's about leaving a lasting impact on the world.

By embracing philanthropy, mentorship, environmental conservation, and knowledge sharing, you contribute to a brighter future for humanity. Your legacy becomes a beacon of hope and inspiration for generations to come.

As you embark on this journey of legacy building and giving back, remember that your actions, no matter how small, can create ripples of positive change. Whether it's supporting education, empowering entrepreneurs, or preserving the environment, your legacy is a testament to your compassion and generosity. Embrace the opportunity to make a difference and leave behind a legacy that not only enriches the lives of others but also illuminates the path toward a more compassionate, equitable, and sustainable world. Stay compassionate, stay engaged, and let your legacy be a testament to the profound impact of a giving heart and a generous spirit.

7.1 CREATING A
LASTING LEGACY:

Creating a lasting legacy is about much more than the wealth amassed during your lifetime; it's about the positive impact you leave on the world and the lives of others. In this section, we delve into the profound importance of defining and nurturing a legacy, extending far beyond financial contributions and reflecting your values, beliefs, and aspirations.

Defining Your Legacy:

- Reflecting on Values: Take time to introspect and identify the core values that define your character. Your legacy should reflect these values, whether they revolve around education, social justice, healthcare, or environmental conservation. Aligning your legacy with your values ensures its authenticity and impact.
- Family and Community: Consider the legacy you want to leave for your family and community. It could be a legacy of education, kindness, or entrepreneurship. Engage your family in discussions about your shared values and the impact you collectively want to make. A shared family legacy creates a sense of purpose and unity.

Educational Endowments:

- Empowering Future Generations: Education is a powerful catalyst for change. By establishing scholarships, endowments, or educational programs, you empower individuals to overcome barriers and reach their full potential. Education provides the tools for personal growth and societal progress.
- Supporting Schools and Universities: Contribute to schools and universities in your community. Enhance infrastructure, fund research programs, or provide financial aid to deserving students. Education institutions play a pivotal role in shaping the leaders and innovators of tomorrow.

Entrepreneurship and Innovation:

- Supporting Entrepreneurs: Foster entrepreneurship by supporting startups and small businesses. Provide mentorship, access to resources, or seed funding. Entrepreneurial ventures drive economic growth and create employment opportunities, fostering innovation and prosperity.
- Innovation Hubs: Establish innovation hubs or coworking spaces that nurture creativity and collaboration. These spaces provide aspiring entrepreneurs with a conducive environment to develop ideas, collaborate, and bring innovative solutions to fruition.

Conclusion: A Legacy of Impact and Inspiration

Creating a lasting legacy is a deeply personal and meaningful endeavor. It is about the positive imprint you leave on the world, shaping the future for generations to come. Your legacy isn't just a testament to your success; it's a beacon of hope, inspiration, and empowerment.

As you define your legacy, remember that it's not confined to grand gestures; it's about the everyday actions that reflect your values and principles. Whether it's supporting education, nurturing entrepreneurship, or championing social causes, your legacy becomes a source of inspiration for others to follow. Embrace the opportunity to make a difference and leave behind a legacy that echoes your compassion, generosity, and commitment to a better world. Stay visionary, stay compassionate, and let your legacy be a testament to the profound impact of a purpose-driven life.

7.2 PHILANTHROPY
AND SOCIAL IMPACT:

Philanthropy and social impact initiatives are powerful vehicles for creating positive change in the world. In this section, we explore the transformative potential of strategic philanthropy and social entrepreneurship, emphasizing the importance of making a meaningful impact in the lives of others and contributing to the betterment of society.

Strategic Philanthropy:

- Identifying Causes: Reflect on the social issues that resonate with your values and beliefs. Whether it's healthcare, poverty alleviation, gender equality, or environmental conservation, choose causes that align with your passions. Focusing your philanthropic efforts allows for concentrated impact.
- Research and Due Diligence: Conduct thorough research on charitable organizations and initiatives. Assess their efficiency, transparency, and impact metrics. Collaborate with reputable organizations that have a track record of making a difference. Due diligence ensures that your contributions are utilized effectively.

Social Entrepreneurship:

- Market-Driven Solutions: Social entrepreneurship involves creating sustainable solutions to societal challenges. By combining business acumen with social consciousness, social entrepreneurs develop enterprises that address pressing issues while remaining financially viable. Support social entrepreneurs and invest in their ventures to fuel innovation and social impact.

- Empowering Communities: Social entrepreneurship empowers communities by providing employment opportunities, skills development, and access to essential services. By supporting social enterprises, you contribute to economic development and poverty reduction, fostering self-reliance and resilience within communities.

Corporate Social Responsibility (CSR):
- Ethical Business Practices: Encourage businesses to adopt ethical practices and social responsibility. CSR initiatives can include environmental conservation, fair labor practices, and community development programs. By promoting CSR, you influence businesses to operate responsibly and contribute positively to society.
- Employee Engagement: Engage employees in philanthropic and volunteer activities. Encourage corporate volunteering, donation matching programs, and community outreach efforts. Engaged employees contribute not only through financial support but also through their time, skills, and expertise, amplifying the impact of CSR initiatives.

Conclusion: Fostering a Compassionate Society
Philanthropy and social impact initiatives are not just acts of generosity; they are catalysts for societal transformation. By actively participating in philanthropy, supporting social entrepreneurs, and advocating for ethical business practices, you contribute to the creation of a compassionate society.

Your involvement in philanthropic efforts extends far beyond monetary contributions; it serves as an inspiration to others, encouraging a culture of giving and empathy. As you engage in philanthropy and social entrepreneurship, you become a beacon of hope, demonstrating the profound impact of compassion and collective action. Stay committed, stay engaged, and let your philanthropic endeavors be a testament to the boundless possibilities of a compassionate and caring society.

7.3 MENTORSHIP AND KNOWLEDGE SHARING:

Mentorship and knowledge sharing are invaluable gifts that empower others to achieve their full potential. In this section, we explore the transformative power of mentorship and the significance of sharing knowledge, experiences, and expertise. By nurturing the next generation of leaders and innovators, you create a legacy of wisdom and inspiration.

Mentoring Future Leaders:

- Guiding Aspiring Entrepreneurs: Share your entrepreneurial journey and insights with aspiring business owners. Mentorship provides guidance, encouragement, and a supportive network, helping entrepreneurs navigate challenges and make informed decisions. Your experiences serve as invaluable lessons.
- Empowering Youth: Mentorship programs for young individuals provide mentorship in various fields, from academics to career planning. By empowering youth, you contribute to their personal and professional development, fostering a generation of confident, capable leaders.

Educational Initiatives:

- Online Learning Platforms: Contribute to online learning platforms by creating courses, tutorials, or educational content. Online education breaks down barriers to learning, making knowledge accessible to people worldwide. Your expertise can inspire learners and equip them with practical skills.
- Guest Lectures and Workshops: Offer guest lectures or workshops at educational institutions. Sharing real-world experiences and industry insights enriches academic learning. Engage with students, encouraging critical thinking and creativity, and inspiring them to pursue their passions.

Authorship and Thought Leadership:

- Writing Books and Articles: Share your knowledge by writing books, articles, or blogs. Authorship allows you to delve into topics deeply, providing comprehensive insights to readers. Whether it's personal finance, entrepreneurship, or self-development, your words can inspire and educate a global audience.
- Public Speaking and Conferences: Participate in public speaking events and conferences. Thought leadership sessions allow you to share your expertise with a diverse audience. Engage in discussions, share innovative ideas, and contribute to thought-provoking conversations that drive positive change.

Conclusion: Fostering Growth and Innovation

Mentorship and knowledge sharing are bridges that connect generations, fostering growth, innovation, and personal development. By being a mentor and sharing your knowledge, you create a ripple effect of positive change. Your guidance provides individuals with the confidence to pursue their dreams and the resilience to overcome challenges.

As you embark on the journey of mentorship and knowledge sharing, remember that your impact extends far beyond the individuals you directly interact with. By empowering others, you contribute to a society enriched with wisdom, creativity, and innovation. Stay open, stay engaged, and let your mentorship and knowledge sharing initiatives be a testament to the enduring legacy of wisdom and guidance.

7.4 SUSTAINABILITY AND ENVIRONMENTAL CONSERVATION:

Sustainability and environmental conservation are integral components of a responsible and compassionate society. In this section, we explore the critical importance of supporting initiatives that promote eco-friendly practices, preserve natural resources, and foster a harmonious relationship between humanity and the environment. By championing sustainability, you contribute to a healthier planet for current and future generations.

Supporting Green Initiatives:
- Renewable Energy Advocacy: Advocate for renewable energy sources such as solar, wind, and hydroelectric power. Support policies and initiatives that promote the transition from fossil fuels to clean energy. Renewable energy reduces carbon emissions and mitigates the impact of climate change.
- Reforestation Projects: Contribute to reforestation efforts by supporting organizations planting trees and restoring degraded forests. Trees play a vital role in absorbing carbon dioxide, purifying the air, and providing habitat for diverse wildlife. Reforestation contributes to biodiversity conservation and climate stability.

Promoting Eco-Friendly Practices:
- Sustainable Agriculture: Support farmers and agricultural practices that prioritize sustainability. Sustainable agriculture techniques minimize the use of harmful chemicals, conserve water, and promote soil health. By endorsing sustainable farming, you encourage environmentally conscious food production.
- Waste Reduction Campaigns: Get involved in waste reduction initiatives within your community. Support recycling programs, organize cleanup events, and promote the responsible disposal of waste. Waste reduction minimizes pollution and conserves natural resources.

Environmental Education:

- Educational Outreach: Engage in environmental education and awareness programs. Raise awareness about climate change, conservation, and sustainable living practices. Education empowers individuals to make informed choices and adopt eco-friendly behaviors, contributing to a culture of environmental consciousness.
- Youth Empowerment: Empower young individuals to become environmental advocates. Support youth-led initiatives, eco-clubs, and environmental projects in schools and communities. Youth engagement fosters a sense of responsibility toward the environment and encourages innovative solutions to environmental challenges.

Conclusion: Preserving Our Planet for Generations to Come

Sustainability and environmental conservation are not just ethical choices; they are imperatives for the survival of our planet. By actively supporting green initiatives, promoting eco-friendly practices, and investing in environmental education, you become a steward of the Earth.

Your efforts, combined with those of countless others, create a collective movement toward a sustainable future. As you champion environmental conservation, remember that every action, no matter how small, contributes to a greener, cleaner, and more sustainable world. Stay committed, stay passionate, and let your dedication to environmental preservation be a beacon of hope for future generations. Together, we can build a world where humanity and nature coexist harmoniously, ensuring a vibrant planet for generations to come.

www.ingramcontent.com/pod-product-compliance
Lightning Source LLC
Chambersburg PA
CBHW072342290526
45794CB00002B/983